HISTORIC HOUSES
of
VIRGINIA

HISTORIC HOUSES
of
VIRGINIA

GREAT PLANTATION HOUSES, MANSIONS,
AND COUNTRY PLACES

KATHRYN MASSON

FOREWORD BY CALDER LOTH
INTRODUCTION BY RICHARD GUY WILSON

PHOTOGRAPHY BY STEVEN BROOKE

RIZZOLI
NEW YORK

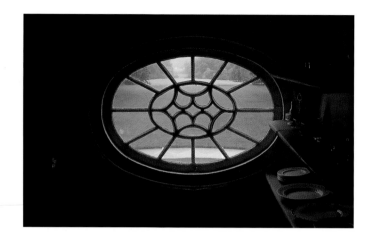

For Frances — K.M.

For Suzanne and Miles — S.B.

First published in the United States of America in 2006 by
RIZZOLI INTERNATIONAL PUBLICATIONS, INC.
300 Park Avenue South, New York, NY 10010
www.rizzoliusa.com

ISBN-10: 0-8478-2861-1
ISBN-13: 9-780847-828616
LCCN: 200692444

FRONT COVER *Mount Vernon (p. 68)*
BACK COVER *Long Branch (p. 194)*

PAGE 1 *Stratford Hall (p. 58)*
PAGE 2 *Oatlands (p. 184)*
PAGE 3 *Virginia state flower, the American dogwood*
PAGE 4 *Mount Vernon window*

DESIGNED BY ABIGAIL STURGES

Printed and bound in China

2006 2007 2008 2009 2010/ 10 9 8 7 6 5 4 3 2 1

CONTENTS

PREFACE

his book was written as a result of a request by Charles Miers, Rizzoli's publisher, for a new book on some of the great houses of Virginia. It was my pleasure to study the possibilities, venture out to discover places new to me in Virginia, and decide on a selection of some of the most beautiful and historic houses in the Commonwealth. The houses were chosen for their diversity of building materials, architectural styles, location, and construction periods, but within the time frame of the early eighteenth to the early nineteenth centuries. Their images are meant, along with a short text and captions, to be a partial representation of Virginia's architectural history, and hopefully to entice the reader to further investigation. The book was then taken to a higher plane with the expertise and generosity of Mr. Calder Loth, Senior Architectural Historian of the Virginia Department of Historic Resources, and Dr. Richard Guy Wilson, Commonwealth Professor and Chair of the Architectural History Department at the University of Virginia in Charlottesville. These two scholars of Virginia's architectural history articulated complicated but fundamental ideas with eloquence and grace. Mr. Loth's Foreword and Dr. Wilson's Introduction are meant to complement each other and my text and they add immeasurably to the understanding and appreciation of these twenty houses and Virginia's architectural history, a priceless part of our American heritage. I cannot thank them enough.

I would also like to acknowledge the ever-outstanding photography of Steven Brooke. His images are full of beauty and insight. Senior Editor of Architecture David Morton and Associate Editor Douglas Curran at Rizzoli Publications have been a pleasure to work with, as always. My husband, David Pashley, has been more than supportive. And during the course of my adventures, it was a pleasure not only to visit these historic houses but to meet the owners of the private residences and the executive directors, curators, public relations and other staff members of the historic house museums. Everyone could not have been more helpful and knowledgeable. My sincere thanks to you all. And since you are so numerous, I have listed everyone in the Acknowledgments. I look forward to learning from you again soon.

OPPOSITE *The finely carved wood orna-mentation throughout the interior at Shirley is original, as are various works of art and eighteenth-century furnishings.*

FOREWORD

CALDER LOTH

Several years ago I served as one of the curators of an exhibition of Virginia architectural drawings for the Virginia Museum of Fine Arts. At that time my colleagues and I made the bold statement that Virginia's greatest contribution to the arts is architecture. I believe that claim is a valid one. When we think of Virginia, we really don't think of poetry, paintings, or music, we think of fine old buildings. Perhaps the most familiar and admired of our architectural achievements are our historic houses. With their refined proportions and decorous detailing, these gracious dwellings appeal to our innate sense of beauty. Though dignified, most also have a homey quality. Most aren't so grand that we can't have the fun of imagining ourselves living in them.

Unlike furniture and paintings, it's all but impossible to collect houses, especially famous ones. And while you can see scores of art objects in an afternoon's stroll through a museum, it's not that easy to visit groups of houses in a set time period. Virginia's historic houses are widely scattered and some remain strictly private. Thus, it's a special treat for architectural aficionados to be able to peruse a presentation of some of our best domestic architecture between the covers of a beautifully illustrated book. With the carefully chosen images and informed text presented here by Kathryn Masson, we can absorb in one sitting the essence of a connoisseur's selection of outstanding examples of the Commonwealth's premier historic houses. This is not the first of such books nor will it be the last, but what sets this one apart is its mix of private residences and museum houses: urban, suburban, and rural, spanning three centuries. Indeed, this is one of the few Virginia architectural anthologies to include important twentieth-century works along with great landmarks of earlier eras. We must start recognizing that fine twentieth-century houses are now historic resources. Milburne, completed in 1935, is among the Commonwealth's most sophisticated examples of twentieth-century Colonial Revival architecture, and is a welcome addition to our architectural legacy. Williamsburg's 1930s reconstructed Governor's Palace holds a unique place in America's roster of twentieth-century buildings.

Virginia has the good fortune to have beautiful houses to show off in a book such as this because many people and organizations have gone to great effort to ensure their survival. The story of Virginia's historic houses is the story of American historic preservation. The preservation movement began in this country with the founding of the Mount Vernon Ladies' Association in 1853 to rescue the home of our first president. The Ladies' action inspired the formation of many other groups such as the Thomas Jefferson Foundation, which acquired Monticello in 1923, and the Robert E. Lee Memorial Association, which purchased Stratford in 1929 and undertook its restoration. The Association for the Preservation of Virginia Antiquities, formed in 1889 as the nation's first statewide preservation organization, has rescued numerous notable houses over more than a century of its existence. The APVA Preservation Virginia has been the custodian of Richmond's John Marshall house since 1911. The National Trust for Historic Preservation holds title to more properties in Virginia than any other state. Oatlands, donated to the trust in 1965, is one of the organization's most important and popular holdings.

Additional organizations, while not guided by a preservation mission specifically, have contributed to the maintenance of Virginia's architectural legacy. Important houses have been sensitively converted to executive retreats, training centers, corporate headquarters, schools, and inns. The columned Carter Hall in the lower Shenandoah Valley, the very image of a stately plantation residence, since 1977 has been the William B. Walsh Education Center and headquarters of Project HOPE. The commodious mansion and its dependencies are made available for meetings, conferences and a variety of other events. Such adaptive new uses allow for greater public enjoyment and have given new life to many noteworthy properties.

The Commonwealth of Virginia, which normally avoids acquiring historic houses as museums, made an exception when in 1932 it accepted ownership of George Mason's Gunston Hall. The long-term restoration of the property has taken place under the patronage of The National Society of The Colonial Dames in America. Most of the historic houses owned by the Commonwealth, however, are official residences and still serve the functions for which they were built. While not necessarily the objects of preservation efforts, many have had to undergo restoration to keep them in use. The state's premier official residence, the Executive Mansion on Richmond's Capitol Square, underwent exterior restoration in the late 1980s when many of its long-missing decorative features were replaced. A comprehensive interior restoration with much-needed upgrades of services was completed in 2000.

Other branches of government have played roles in the preservation of Virginia's historic houses. The federal government has been most active in securing historic dwellings associated with Civil War battlefields and other patriotic sites. However, it also has been responsible for the restoration and exhibition of Arlington, one of America's most conspicuous historic mansions, dominating the heights overlooking Arlington National Cemetery and Washington, D.C. Nearby in Alexandria, the Northern Virginia Regional Park Authority undertook as a Bicentennial project the restoration of the Carlyle house, long hidden by surrounding later buildings.

One of the nation's most ambitious historic preservation projects has been the restoration of Virginia's colonial capital by the Colonial Williamsburg Foundation. Beginning in the 1920s, the Foundation has restored some eighty of the town's historic structures, rescuing many from dereliction. Equally important, the Foundation undertook the reconstruction of certain key buildings lost over time. Conspicuous among these was the Governor's Palace, begun in 1706 and destroyed by fire in 1781. The reconstructed palace, based on meticulous scholarship and archaeological evidence, was completed in 1934 and has since become a key symbol of America's colonial history and a focal point of the Williamsburg restoration.

A very different twentieth-century historic landmark is Virginia House, in Richmond's Windsor Farms neighborhood. It was built in the late 1920s with architectural elements salvaged from Warwick Priory, a late-medieval English structure purchased by Ambassador and Mrs. Alexander Weddell when threatened with demolition. The Weddells bequeathed the house and its extensive gardens to the Virginia Historical Society, which exhibits the estate, both as an expression of the 1920s American county house movement and as a reminder of Virginia's English antecedents.

Virginia has benefited from many private individuals who have devoted time and treasure to securing historic houses. Julian Wood Glass insured the future of his 1794 ancestral home, Glen Burnie, in Winchester, when he established the Glass-Glen Burnie Foundation, which has exhibited the house and Glass's outstanding collection of art and antiques since 1992. In nearby Clarke County, the late Harry Z. Isaacs in 1986 purchased the great antebellum mansion, Long Branch, and established a foundation to use the property as a cultural center and to show off the house with his collection of decorative arts. Virginia's venerable Carter family has long recognized its special mission to share with the public their famous ancestral home Shirley with its many generations of family possessions. This James River plantation, seat of the Carters and their ancestors since the 1650s, is a remarkable demonstration of family continuity and stewardship.

The late Malcolm Jamieson devoted most of his life to the restoration and exhibition of his home Berkeley, one of Virginia's great colonial mansions and birthplace of a signer of the Declaration of Independence and a president of the United States. Jamieson was also one of the state's first individuals to secure through legal means the future of his property by donating a permanent preservation easement on Berkeley to the Commonwealth of Virginia. Such sense of stewardship has been a prime motivator for the preservation of numerous privately owned historic houses. Over the past forty years more than three hundred preservation easements, the majority on historic residences, have been voluntarily donated to the Commonwealth through the Board of Historic Resources. These easements offer permanent legal protection from demolition and inappropriate change. Moreover, easements also serve to protect the settings of rural houses by prohibiting the commercial development of associated acreage.

Preservation easements have been the leading tool for safeguarding Virginia's historic properties as they ensure the integrity of places despite changes of use and ownership. In addition to Berkeley, three of the six private residences featured in this book—Eyre Hall, Mount Airy, and Tuckahoe—are protected with voluntarily donated easements. Both Eyre Hall and Mount Airy are still owned by their original families. Tuckahoe has been carefully tended by three generations of the same family since the 1930s. These places are among the nation's most stellar examples of colonial architecture. Berkeley, Mount Airy, and Tuckahoe are National Historic Landmarks. Eyre Hall is being proposed for NHL designation. We can be thankful that their owners recognize that these properties are important not just to them and their families, but also to all Americans. We owe much gratitude to them as well as to all the owners and custodians of the wonderful places Kathryn Masson has chosen to share with us for keeping these treasures alive.

INTRODUCTION

Richard Guy Wilson

*F*or many Americans the word *Virginia* invokes a variety of images and associations. These can range from an I-64/95 glimpse of pastoral countryside settings, a distant view of Richmond's skyline, or an evocation of names and places—Jamestown, Yorktown, Williamsburg, Mount Vernon, Monticello, Bull Run, Appomattox. Waves of history well up from Virginia's soil. Places and buildings help create memory. They are the tangible elements—in some cases transferred into symbols—that make a physical reality of the storied past.

The houses shown in this book, from the large redbrick plantations such as Shirley to the wood-sided, extended form of Eyre Hall or the giant columns of Arlington House, represent different strains of Virginia's history. They are a selection—not a complete survey—of important Virginia houses. Many of these houses might be considered as archetypically Virginian in that they date from the 1720s to the 1830s. The

exceptions to this—Virginia House, Milburne, and the Governor's Palace—which were built in the 1920s and 1930s—largely follow the Virginia image in that they evoke or revive a storied, or even a fictional, earlier time. To paraphrase the great southern novelist William Faulkner: history is not over in Virginia, the past isn't really even past.

The Commonwealth of Virginia (the official title) as a geographical entity lies in the mid-Atlantic region and contains a variety of topographies. There are the many wide rivers and waterways, such as the Potomac, the James, the York, the Rappahannock, and the Chesapeake Bay, which were the early transportation routes and bisect the low lying sometimes marshy Tidewater and Eastern Shore areas. Next is the hilly Piedmont, the mountains—Blue Ridge and Alleghenies—and the great valley, the Shenandoah, along with large and medium sized cities, small hamlets, and bucol-

PRECEDING PAGES *The bucolic scene above Paris in Fauquier County is one of the most beautiful in Virginia.*

OPPOSITE BOTTOM *The church tower at Historic Jamestowne was rescued from destruction by the early members of APVA Preservation Virginia. It dates to about 1647. Historic Jamestowne is open to the public as a historic site and is co-administered by the National Park Service and APVA Preservation Virginia.*

ABOVE *Bacon's Castle, located in Surry County, was built in 1665 and is one of only a few surviving examples of Jacobean domestic architecture in America. It is preserved and interpreted by APVA Preservation Virginia and is open to the public as a historic site.* Photo courtesy of APVA Preservation Virginia.

OPPOSITE TOP *The earliest English settlements and plantations were established along the James River, seen here from Tuckahoe.*

ic rural scenes where time appears to have stopped. Initially the largest of the original thirteen states, Virginia stretched all the way to the Mississippi; in 1784 Kentucky and portions of other states were carved off. What is now West Virginia remained as part of the Commonwealth until 1863 when it seceded—with a little Union help—during the Civil War.

Virginia, named for the "Virgin Queen" Elizabeth I, was in 1607 the site of the first permanent English settlement in the New World at Jamestown. One of the first American legends begins here—the story of Pocahontas, her father Chief Powhatan, and Captain John Smith—a nice tale but which contains only fragments of truth. It is fact that the displacement of the original native inhabitants, the Indians, began at Jamestown; and it is also true that Jamestown saw, early on, the creation of a new culture and architecture. During the seventeenth and eighteenth centuries, Virginia, with its tobacco production, became one of the most prosperous colonies in America and also the largest slaveholder among the original British colonies. Williamsburg replaced Jamestown in 1699 as the colony's capital and, during the 1770s, from its taverns, houses, and public buildings emerged many of the themes of secession and ultimately revolt from England and the quest for independence. Battles were fought on its soil and the final victory over the British took place at Yorktown in 1781 when Lord Cornwallis surrendered to General George Washington. In Richmond, the

new state capital after 1779, Thomas Jefferson designed in 1785 the new state house modeled on the ancient Roman temple at Nimes, France. This was the first major American public building after the Revolution and Jefferson's design helped establish classicism as the image we associate with governmental architecture.

Virginia's prominence in early American history is apparent in the fact that four of the first five presidents came from Virginia and it was the birthplace of four more. The state's prosperity began to give out in the 1820s and although Virginians would continue—and many still do today—to maintain a socially elitist stance toward the rest of the United States, they fell on hard times as the land gave out because of overproduction of tobacco. Unwilling to embrace the new industrialism of the North, the state turned inward: to be a Virginian, as Robert E. Lee demonstrated, was more important than to be an American. Richmond served as the capital of the Confederacy during the Civil War and Virginia became the central battleground of that conflict. Virginia embraced industrialism after the War but resisted the emancipation of the former slaves, enacting Jim Crow laws and instituting segregation. A mythology of a noble colonial past complete with big red brick plantation houses and happy slaves in the fields along with the nobility of the Confederate cause became a mainstay of American mythology until the civil rights movement of the 1950s and 1960s. Today Virginia resembles much of the United States—strip malls, burgeoning suburbs, too many cars—and yet the countryside and the older buildings help it to retain its special character.

Most of the houses shown in this book date from the hallowed time period when Virginia ruled the country, that is, the eighteenth and early nineteenth century, and the years that historians sometimes label as Colonial, Georgian, or Federal in chronology. Located for the most part along large rivers, tributaries, or bays, which allowed for shipment of tobacco and other produce, they were the plantation manors of the large landowners. The few exceptions to plantations, such as wealthy tobacco merchant John Carlyle's house in Alexandria and John Marshall's house and the Executive (Governor's) mansion both in Richmond, were located in major trading centers and were also homes of the elite.

These large houses mostly built of brick with a few of timber were the exception for their time, since most Virginians

OPPOSITE *Pear Valley, owned by APVA Preservation Virginia, is one of the few remaining original wood dwellings that exhibits a vernacular design typical of eighteenth-century Virginia. Photo courtesy of APVA Preservation Virginia.*

ABOVE *Burwell Cemetery and Chapel, or "Old Chapel" in Millwood, constructed in 1793 of local limestone, is believed to be the oldest Episcopal church building west of the Blue Ridge Mountains. The renowned Bishop Meade spoke here as a young minister. Members of many prominent eighteenth-century Virginia families are buried in its cemetery.*

LEFT *Historic Christ Church, in Lancaster County, was built c. 1735 by Robert "King" Carter, and is one of the most substantial and well-designed buildings of its era. The scale and proportions of the interior together with its vaulted ceiling and handsome woodwork create an exceedingly graceful space. It is preserved today through the efforts of the Foundation for Historic Christ Church, Inc.*

RIGHT *Unassuming rural backroads such as this are found throughout Virginia's countryside.*

BELOW *The c. 1782 Burwell-Morgan Mill in Millwood, Clarke County, was built as a commercial enterprise and is the centerpiece of the charming hamlet. Now restored and working, it hosts tours and events such as the fall regional art show.*

OPPOSITE TOP *Unspoiled and protected from development, the c. 1733 village of Waterford is a National Historic Landmark District in Loudoun County. Normally a quiet community of artists and writers, it comes alive once a year during its October fair. Produced by the Waterford Foundation, the juried fair's proceeds are used to protect and purchase sites.*

OPPOSITE BOTTOM *James Madison's Montpelier, whose restoration is set for completion in 2008, is a National Trust historic site administered by the Montpelier Foundation. In its two-acre formal garden, restored by The Garden Club of Virginia, traces of Madison's original garden survive in the plan of paths and parterres and various original trees.*

lived much more modestly. The state was largely rural and small houses, farm outbuildings, and mills were the dominant presence, with here and there a church. The brick Christ Church at Lancaster, still extant, was one of the largest religious structures in the colonies; most churches were small, of wood, and have disappeared. A few courthouses dotted the landscape and they were not usually in a town but at a central crossroads for the county they served. The only other nearby structure might be a tavern and the county land-recorder's office.

Although the archaeology at Jamestown has revealed stone foundations, some large-building footings, and wooden flooring dating to 1610, along with the remains of a church tower, the typical Virginia house of the seventeenth, eighteenth, and early nineteenth centuries was a single- or two-room affair built out of wood and frequently with a dirt floor. Because of

their perishability very few of these houses survive. Of the native Indians who also inhabited the landscape nothing remains but a few poignant prints of their settlements and dwellings along with some archaeological fragments. Also, almost completely vanquished is the housing of the extensive slave population who worked the plantations and who also served in the large houses. The African-American housing was equally modest and perishable. Somewhat larger were the dwellings of some towns such as Waterford with its free standing buildings or Alexandria's row houses, but Virginia's economy was agrarian and that myth of the power—along with the virtue—of the countryside still holds today.

Architecturally many of the large houses in this book indicate a loose indebtedness to English pattern books in their form, plan, and details. This is illuminated in the tendency toward symmetry on the main entrance façade, balance and

prints might have served as a source. Reference to such materials was certainly part of the process by which Thomas and Hannah Ludwell Lee and George and Martha Washington created Stratford Hall (circa 1734) and Mount Vernon (circa 1757) respectively. With Washington we know some of the books he owned such as Abraham Swan's *British Architect* and Colin Campbell's *Vitruvius Britannicus*. William Buckland, an indentured joiner/carver to George Mason, either used Mason's pattern books, or perhaps brought his own when he arrived in Fairfax County in 1755 and began embellishing the interiors of Gunston Hall. Employing the pattern books of Batty Langley, Buckland created some of the most lavish and sophisticated interiors on this side of the Atlantic.

While growing out of this owner/builder tradition with his own house Monticello, which was under frequent modification and redesign between 1769 and 1809, Thomas Jefferson became in a sense a full fledged architect with his designs for the Richmond Capitol, several county court houses, houses for friends (such as the portico at Montpelier), and the University of Virginia. The university expresses Jefferson's fondness for the Italian architect Palladio for, as a friend remembered, "With Mr. Jefferson I conversed at length on the subject of architecture—'Palladio,' he said, 'was the Bible—you should get it and stick close to it.'" Jefferson owned the largest architectural library in the young nation and from his books, his experience with building, and observations (he spent 1784–89 abroad), Jefferson trained himself as an architect. Jefferson's importance to American architecture cannot be overstated.

Jefferson's death in 1826 symbolically indicates the end of Virginia's prominence. The soil was worn out and economically the state stagnated. A few grand houses were built after 1830 but in comparison to elsewhere in the South, Virginia has few large Greek Revival houses; it becomes a backwater. The Victorian period and the early twentieth century did produce some grand houses but the key feature is a retrospective turning back to the past and reinventing it. Seeking a historical legitimacy to counter the diminishment of the state's status, Virginians constructed a new landscape peopled with statues of Colonial and Confederate heroes. They even looked to sources that dated earlier than Virginia's founding or to "Olde England." A modest trade grew up of purchasing fragments of English buildings that dated to the twelfth though the sixteenth centuries and reconstructing them along the James River such

regularity of parts, and employment of classical ornament around doorways, windows, and on the interior in the form of moldings. Eighteenth-century planters were rich and they liked to show off their wealth and sophistication. The classicism incipient in the architecture of the time marks one of the major differences with that of the seventeenth century and houses such as Bacon's Castle (circa 1665 and later), which while balanced has Jacobean details. In most cases the imposing houses of the eighteenth century were a joint product of the owner and his/her builders. It should be noted that, while the female role in the building of the grand houses is frequently overlooked, women certainly played an influential role. Their dowries paid many of the bills and, as a result, often they could rule what happened inside. Much of the interior at Mount Vernon was supervised by Martha Washington while her husband was off fighting the war. House owners might have owned or had access to pattern books, or in some cases

OPPOSITE *Town houses in Alexandria are as sophisticated and charming now as when they were constructed in the eighteenth-century urban center.*

ABOVE *The University of Virginia in Charlottesville was founded by Thomas Jefferson in 1819 as his Academical Village. With its Rotunda and original pavilions designed by Jefferson, it is arguably one of the most beautiful campuses in America.*

LEFT *The Virginia State Capitol in Richmond, completed in 1788, was designed by Thomas Jefferson based on the temple form. His inspiration was the Maison Carrée in Nimes. Photo by John O. Peters for the Virginia Department of Historic Resources.*

as the Wendells did at Virginia House in Richmond. This gave them a pedigree dating back to the Tudors and ever earlier. More specifically tied to the native soil were the elegant red-brick James River plantation houses designed by architects such as William Lawrence Bottomley of New York which first sprouted up along Monument Avenue in Richmond and came to dot the Virginia countryside. The Colonial Williamsburg Restoration, or more properly "reconstruction" of the later 1920s and 1930s (and still continuing) brought even more to prominence Virginia's historical architecture. Funded by one of the world's wealthiest individuals, John D. Rockefeller II, and widely and heavily promoted, buildings such as the Governor's Palace entered the national imagination. Williamsburg was a twentieth century version of what the colonial period should have been like: neat houses and gardens all furnished with immaculate antiques or reproductions. Colonial Williamsburg became one of the great—perhaps the greatest—tastemakers of twentieth century America.

The houses of Virginia as selected and shown in this book are a great national treasure. They have housed many people of different races and they tell many stories. They are also models of a period of design that illuminates the diversity possible and a standard of taste hard to surpass.

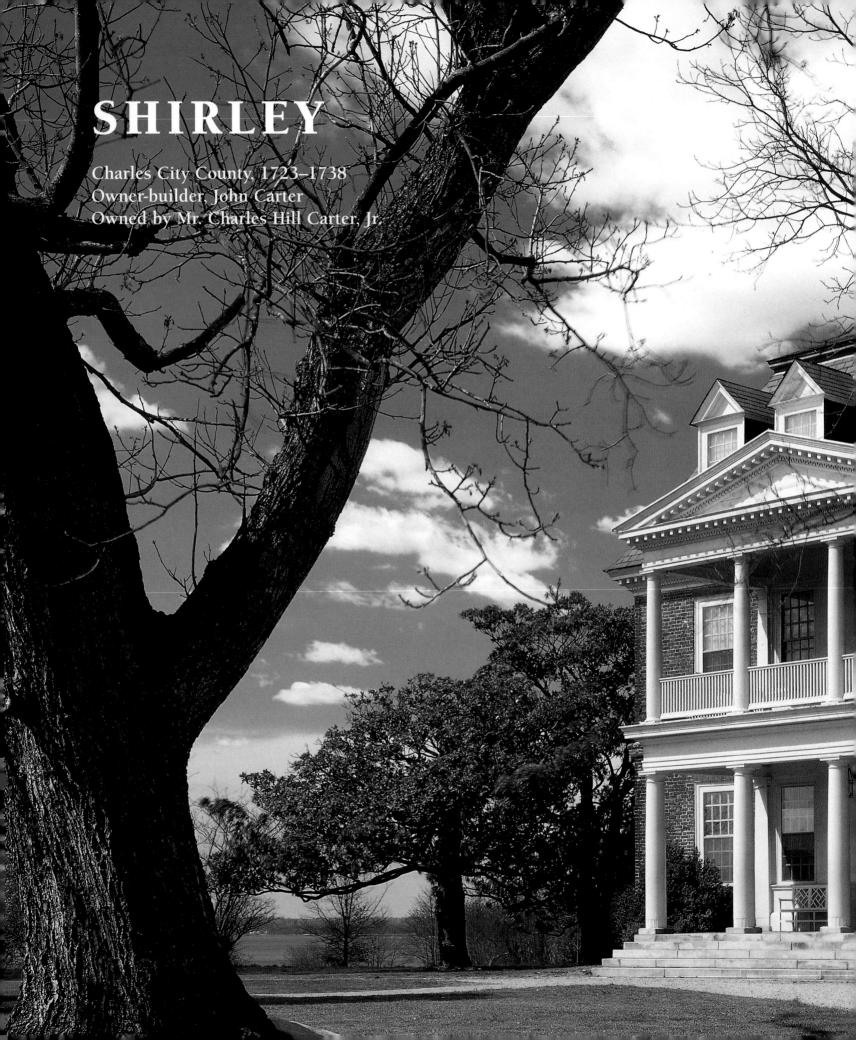

SHIRLEY

Charles City County, 1723–1738
Owner-builder, John Carter
Owned by Mr. Charles Hill Carter, Jr.

PRECEDING PAGES *Shirley, a National Historic Landmark, is one of the most intact and beautiful eighteenth-century plantations in Virginia. Its stately English architecture is reminiscent of the Governor's Palace in Williamsburg. The mansion was built by John Carter from 1723 to 1738, with later exterior alterations and interior remodeling. The estate has remained in the hands of the Carter and Hill families for eleven generations.*

RIGHT *Shirley, with its spectacular 350-year-old willow oak at the front entrance, is a stone's throw from the James River. Because of its strategic position near the river, Shirley has been the center of social activity and commerce for its earliest owners, a communication center during the Revolutionary War, and a war zone during the Civil War. Today, Shirley's thriving social life involves annual visitation of over 50,000 and an annual calendar full of fundraisers and special events.*

The architecture of Shirley is exquisitely simple and strong. Brick buildings that have survived for almost 300 years remain in their original configuration of a courtyard focused on a three-story mansion residence, a study in English style similar to the Governor's Palace in Williamsburg. Today there is an austere beauty to this small community of structures, approached through an allée of oak trees, resting at the very water's edge of the James River. This peaceful scene contrasts with its earlier life as a thriving plantation on one of the busiest waterways in early America.

The story of Shirley is that of two famous Virginia families, the Hills and the Carters, intertwined with the Byrds, Lees, and Randolphs, beginning in Virginia's earliest era of unstable settlement. Strategically located on the James River, Shirley has known several incarnations, including that of a vast plantation that created a luxurious life for its owners and heirs, as a communication center during the Revolutionary War in which owners of Shirley became patriots for the emerging new country, and in a war zone during battles of the Civil War.

OPPOSITE *The spectacular walnut cantilevered staircase rises three stories from its base in the front entry hall. In this gracious room with its original decorative paneling and carved architectural detailing, family portraits include those of Edward Hill III, his son Edward Hill IV, and the mother of young Edward, Elizabeth Williams Hill.*

ABOVE *Robert E. Lee's parents were married in this parlor. The intricately carved mantel is one of the most beautiful in any eighteenth-century house. Curved white oak leaves were carved from a single white oak log by master craftsmen, with acorn decoration applied.*

FOLLOWING PAGES *The refined Georgian detailing in the formal dining room's woodwork includes the broken pediment over the doorway. The room features the original Carter family silver.*

Sir Thomas West, third Baron De la Warr, founded West and Sherley Hundred in 1613 for the purpose of creating a tobacco plantation, and by 1616 tobacco was exported from there to England. In 1638 Edward Hill I was granted 450 acres of this plantation, and he increased the size of this holding over the years through marriage and acquisition. In 1700 Edward Hill III inherited the land, and in 1723 his son-in-law John Carter began construction of the brick buildings of Shirley near the former Hill house. In 1738 John Carter and his wife Elizabeth Hill Carter moved into their new residence. The compound was extensive and formally planned, with the large dwelling house set amidst outbuildings including a two-story kitchen with living quarters, a two-story laundry with

living quarters, a granary, an ice house, a large storehouse, and a charming dove cote.

Close proximity to Jamestown, Williamsburg, and Richmond insured Shirley's importance as a communication center and hub of society. Stories of the genteel life of its owners epitomize Virginia hospitality. The Hills and Carters were well known throughout the county for their generosity, even extending their kindness to Union soldiers while Shirley served as a field hospital during the Civil War. General McClellen's thank you note of July 11, 1862, to Mr. Hill Carter attests to this: " . . . my thanks for the noble spirit of humanity you have shown toward men whom you probably regard as bitter foes. . . . "

PRECEDING PAGES *The dovecote at Shirley is beautiful in its simplicity. The complex also includes a smokehouse, pump house, root cellar, and stable. All of these structures are original to Shirley.*

LEFT AND BELOW *Dependency buildings at Shirley are constructed within a forecourt. The forecourt includes a two-story kitchen and a two-story laundry building located closest to the great house. The buildings face and mirror each other in size, dimension, and floor plan. The next two buildings leading away from the great house are one-and-a-half-story, L-shaped service buildings that include the ice house, whose loft served as a granary, and the tool barn, also used as a large storehouse. These two service buildings face and mirror each other in size, dimension, and floor plan.*

Shirley's owners managed the plantation with, and later without, slave labor through times of economic success and through poverty, always keeping the ownership of Shirley at heart. When two sisters produced no heirs to carry on the family heritage, their first cousin once removed (or cousin's son), Charles Hill Carter, Jr., was named heir. This tenth generation member of the Carter family owns Shirley today, an estate admired as an exquisite and flawless vision of eighteenth-century Georgian architecture and for its completeness as an intact James River plantation complex.

BERKELEY

Charles City County, 1726
Architectural designer, Benjamin Harrison IV
Owned by the Jamieson Family

PRECEDING PAGES *Berkeley, or Berkeley's Hundred as it was originally known, is one of the oldest of the James River plantations. Benjamin Harrison IV and his wife Anne Carter Harrison built the Georgian manor house in 1726 as the centerpiece of their plantation. Ten acres of formal gardens that include boxwood parterres and a spreading lawn lead from the back of the house to the banks of the river.*

RIGHT *Built in 1726, the stately brick manor house has withstood the ravages of history for the better part of three centuries. Substantial underpinnings of the house that include huge timbers and a three-foot-thick brick foundation have insured the building's fortitude. The Jamieson family, owners of the national treasure since 1907, have restored and maintained the National Historic Landmark, open to the public, with great care.*

Berkeley, or Berkeley's Hundred as it was originally known, is one of the oldest of the James River plantations. Its stately brick manor house and dependency buildings form the nucleus of what is still a sizeable estate. From the house, an expansive vista begins with an English boxwood allée that leads down a gradual slope through sets of parterred gardens and lawns to the quietly moving river's shore. Surrounding fields and woodlands complete the picturesque setting.

In 1619 a small group of English investors, The Berkeley Company, chartered 8,000 acres of land alongside the James River in Virginia to be settled and farmed for profit. It was on Berkeley's Hundred that the thirty-eight Englishmen who came to settle it held a ceremony for their safe landing, the first Thanksgiving on what would become American shores. The plantation was farmed until an attack by Native Americans in 1622 obliterated the entire enterprise, but was brought back to life as a commercial shipyard by Benjamin Harrison III in 1691. His son Benjamin Harrison IV and his wife Anne Carter built the sturdy three-story Georgian manor house in 1726 as the centerpiece of the plantation. Following the example of Anne's father, the wealthy colonist Robert "King" Carter, the Harrisons became successful tobacco planters, exporting their share of Virginia's main cash crop to England from their estate's wharf.

The Harrisons of Berkeley became one of the most prominent landed families in the colonies. Illustrious Harrison men
included Benjamin V, who, after inheriting Berkeley at eighteen and completing his education at the College of William
and Mary, became active in politics, signed the Declaration of
Independence, and served as the Governor of Virginia three
times. His younger son, William Henry Harrison, became
nationally prominent as the Governor of the Northwest
Territory or what would become Indiana, Ohio, and Illinois.
Known for his victory at the Battle of Tippecanoe, he coined
the first political campaign slogan and won the election to
become the ninth president of the United States in 1841.
From 1889 to 1893, William Henry Harrison's grandson,
Benjamin Harrison, served as the twenty-third President of
the United States.

OPPOSITE *The wide entry hall, with front and back
doors that may be opened to the breezes in the sum-
mer, contains the type of beautiful classically styled
ornamentation that is found throughout the house.*

ABOVE *The formal dining room contains fine eighteenth and early-nineteenth-century furnishings such
as the mahogany sideboard. A portrait of William
Henry Harrison, ninth president of the United States,
hangs over the mantel.*

During the Civil War, General George McClellan occupied Berkeley as his headquarters and his encampment of 140,000 Union soldiers covered the plantation's grounds. After the war, Berkeley mansion, deteriorating from misuse, was saved from complete ruin when John Jamieson, with memories of the great house while encamped there as a drummer boy for McClellan, purchased it in 1907. His son, Malcolm, after inheriting the mansion and 1,400 acres in 1927, and his wife Grace then devoted their knowledge, skill, and funds to the estate's more comprehensive restoration. The substantial underpinnings of the house—huge timbers in the basement ceiling and three-foot-thick brick foundation walls—have insured the building's fortitude while the generosity of the Jamiesons has returned Berkeley to its eighteenth-century splendor and made it available for the public to enjoy.

OPPOSITE AND ABOVE *In 1790, at the suggestion of Thomas Jefferson, Benjamin Harrison VI installed wide double arches that created two great rooms. The width of the double fireplaces and chimneys created useful space under the arches.*

FOLLOWING PAGES *A room at the side of the house on the main level was used at various times as both a bed chamber and the office of Benjamin V, signer of the Declaration of Independence.*

A full quarter of a mile of path leads from the manor house to the James River, through ten acres of landscaped gardens that serve as the site for special events throughout the year. The spectacular "Virginia's First Thanksgiving Festival," held annually, celebrates the 1619 landing of colonists at Berkeley Hundred, who in praise held America's first official Thanksgiving ceremony.

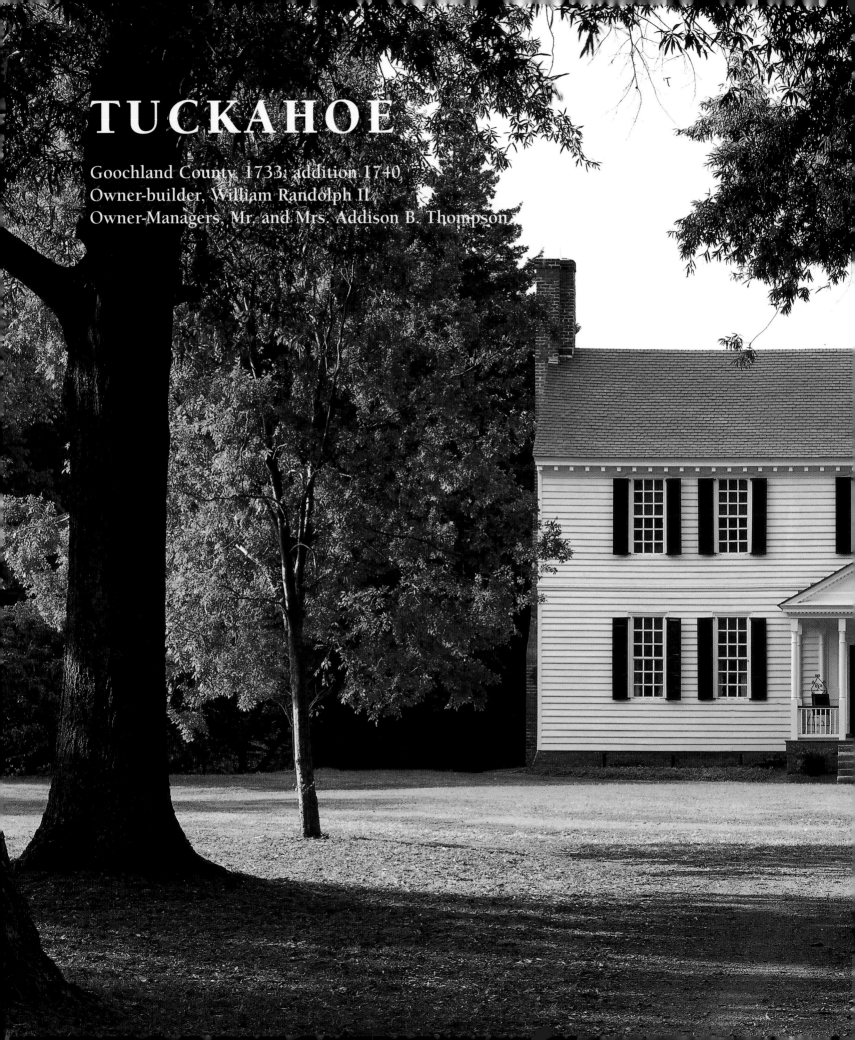

TUCKAHOE

Goochland County, 1733; addition 1740
Owner-builder, William Randolph II
Owner-Managers, Mr. and Mrs. Addison B. Thompson

PRECEDING PAGES *Tuckahoe, a National Historic Landmark, was built in 1733 by William Randolph II and his wife Maria Judith Page (Randolph) of Rosewell. Its form was expanded in 1740 with the addition of a two-story structure, the south wing, and a connecting saloon, making the house H-shaped. Overlooking the fields of the James River bottomlands, with the river in the distance, the main house, dependencies, formal gardens, and landscaping and pastures form one of the most complete colonial plantation complexes in America.*

ABOVE *A schoolhouse built after Peter Jefferson arrived in 1745 became the site where young Thomas Jefferson and his Randolph cousins were tutored. Thomas Jefferson spent seven years at Tuckahoe before returning to his birthplace of Shadwell near Charlottesville. The schoolhouse has an unusual domed plaster ceiling.*

RIGHT *The unassuming architecture of Tuckahoe contrasts with its magnificent interior woodwork. While the design is simple, its many fine and subtle exterior details such as the modillioned cornice, the wood belt course at the second floor level, the Flemish bond brickwork on all of the chimneys and on the eastern and western elevations of the south wing, and the wide muntins in the nine-over-nine-light sash windows give it a timeless grace.*

uckahoe, on a bluff overlooking the James River, is a beautiful and evocative relic of colonial American history. Its importance is due to both its fine architecture and the distinguished Virginians who lived there. It is most widely remembered as the boyhood home of Thomas Jefferson, but its appearance is a product of its association with the venerable Randolph family.

As verified through studies of its structural wood members, construction of the house began in 1733 by William Randolph II, whose grandfather patented the land in 1695. The oldest section, the north wing, was built as a freestanding residence with a center passage and flanking rooms on both levels. In 1740 the house was expanded into an "H"

plan, an architectural form employed in English country houses during the Jacobean era. A new, finely paneled saloon connected the original north wing to a new two-story south wing. The original exterior weatherboarding, Flemish bond brickwork on the chimneys of the north wing and the brick ends of the south wing and the glorious interior woodwork exist today. The white drawing room's paneling was painted in the nineteenth century, but the "burnt" room, the east parlor in the north wing has original unpainted walnut paneling—one of the few Virginia houses to do so. The north stair woodwork is also indigenous black walnut.

William Randolph was the cousin of Jane Randolph, who married Peter Jefferson. Their son was Thomas Jefferson. When William, a widower with three children, died at age thirty-two in 1745, he left instructions designating his friend and in-law, Peter Jefferson, as guardian of his family. Thomas Jefferson was almost two years old when Peter and Jane moved their family from their home near Charlottesville to live at Tuckahoe and raise the Randolph children with their

PRECEDING PAGES *The east parlor or library of the original north wing is known as the "burnt room" because, as legend has it, a torch thrown in by a jealous lover during a wedding ceremony scorched the wall. Although fully paneled as was the style between 1725 and 1750, the unusual design includes rare early carved pilasters with Corinthian capitals and built-in cupboards flanking the fireplace, which now has an early-nineteenth-century mantel. It is one of the finest rooms in the house.*

OPPOSITE *Deep arches at the far ends of the saloon give access to the stairhalls, as shown here in the north wing. Rich walnut paneling as well as heart pine floorboards create warmth and luxury and enhance the late Stuart character of the north hall.*

ABOVE *With a collection of fine antique furnishings and artwork handed down through generations, the grand 30-foot-long, 19-foot-wide pine-paneled saloon resonates with family history. Beyond the arch is the staircase of the north hall with its magnificently carved newel post and stair landing fascia. The crisp distinct forms of a spiral of vines and flowers on the newel post and leavy scrolls surrounding a basket of flowers on the landing's fascia denote the work of a highly skilled artisan.*

ABOVE *The walnut paneling in the west parlor of the north wing was believed to have been painted white by Gabriella Harvie, the second wife of Thomas Mann Randolph I, whose infant son inherited Tuckahoe in 1793. The mantel, added later, is set off by the rest of the room's minimal architectural detailing. Today, the Thompsons' collection of miniature Napoleonic portraits and various French decorative pieces complement the Louis Seize furnishings upholstered in Aubusson tapestry.*

RIGHT *In the dining room two original closets flanking the fireplace, one with a door cut out for an easy passage to the separate kitchen building, are now pantries. The window glass, etched with the names of various visitors, is original, while the mantel is an 1820 addition. The fine antique furnishings of the Thompson family are serviceable and elegant.*

FOLLOWING PAGES *It is believed that the east room on the second floor of the north wing was Thomas Jefferson's bedroom. While the Jeffersons lived in the north wing, it is thought that the Randolph children lived in the south wing. The mantel in the Jefferson bedroom has a flat marble facing surrounded by a simple molding, consistent with those designs of the eighteenth century. If not original to the house, it is of the period.*

own. During their residence at Tuckahoe, Thomas Jefferson, his cousin Thomas Mann Randolph I, and their siblings were educated in the small schoolhouse that still stands adjacent to the main house. By 1754 Peter Jefferson had moved back home but continued to help manage Tuckahoe from afar, as Thomas Mann Randolph I was only eleven years old. It appears that Thomas Jefferson remained at Tuckahoe and was tutored alongside his cousin. As a result of Peter Jefferson's death in 1757, management of the plantation was probably turned over to the sixteen-year-old Thomas Mann Randolph I.

Years later, as was often the case in Virginia, cousins from prominent families intermarried. Thomas Jefferson's daughter Martha married Thomas Mann Randolph I's son and lived with their twelve children with or near Jefferson through much of the remainder of his life.

STRATFORD HALL

Westmoreland County, c. 1738
Architect unknown
Owned and operated by the Robert E. Lee Memorial Association, Inc.

PRECEDING PAGES *Stratford Hall on the Northern Neck is the family seat of the Lees. The commanding brick edifice was built by Thomas Lee in the late 1730s. The plantation includes the great house, four dependency buildings, a coach house, and stables. Stratford Hall is the birthplace of General Robert E. Lee.*

ABOVE *The Great Hall of Stratford is an impressive twenty-nine-foot-square central room with a beautiful 17-foot-high tray ceiling. Windows and doors on all sides allowed full ventilation in this elegant room, used as the family's main entertainment and public reception space. Originals and reproductions of family portraits are hung high on the fully paneled walls that were repainted in 2005 with custom-blended paint in the historically accurate, complex blue-grey-green color.*

Stratford Hall is the seat of one of Virginia's most illustrious founding families, the Lees. Thomas Lee constructed the immense brick house overlooking the Potomac River in the late 1730s from which he ran his tobacco plantation. An entrepreneurial spirit helped Lee increase the wealth originally made by his grandfather, Richard Lee I, an English emigrant who had risen to political power, social prominence, and great wealth early in the seventeenth century.

Thomas Lee would become an important figure in the early days of the colonies. In 1744 he served as one of the commissioners that negotiated the Treaty of Lancaster with the Six Nations of the Iroquois. This decision would later help open the Ohio Valley frontier to English settlement, and

in 1747 Lee would speculate on land to the west as a founder of the Ohio Company. His distinguished political career included service as Justice of Westmoreland, a member of the House of Burgesses, and Naval Officer of the Potomac. He would later have a seat on the Council of State and would be the colony's acting governor. Lee family members would become outstanding American patriots, including Thomas's sons Richard Henry and Francis Lightfoot, who would sign the Declaration of Independence, Henry "Light Horse Harry" who would become a colonel in the Revolutionary War and later governor of Virginia, and his son Robert E. Lee, born at Stratford Hall in 1807, who would become one of America's most illustrious military heroes.

ABOVE *The parlor, located off the west passage, was enlarged c. 1790 by moving its west wall toward the upper stair passage. Its Federal-style detailing reflects the fashion of the day. Today the room is furnished with a bookcase owned by Robert E. Lee's mother-in-law. The portrait over the mantel, attributed to Gilbert Stuart, is Henry "Light Horse Harry" Lee, the Revolutionary War hero and father of Robert E. Lee.*

FOLLOWING PAGES *The dining room, in the east section of the house, contains a large arch that separates it from the cherry tree room. The dining room is furnished with eighteenth-century pieces that include a large drop-leaf table, a set of walnut Queen Anne chairs, and a gilt-framed looking glass. Portraits on the walls include Ludwell family members, and the full-length portrait in the cherry tree room is Queen Caroline.*

Construction of Stratford Hall began after 1737. Over the next few years around 600,000 bricks were fired on site and a mansion was constructed that would be the new residence of Thomas and Hannah Ludwell Lee. The "great house" is a massive two-story brick structure whose unique design conveys status, strength, and solidity. The building is 90 feet wide, approached from the south by a flat plane that gives it an impressive perspective. It is the centerpiece of a quadrant of free-standing out buildings that, taken together, increase the visual impact with an expanse of 200 feet. Formal gardens on either side planted in square perimeters repeat the substantial box shape of the overall plan. The reconstruction of unusual splayed stone steps leads up to the elevated main level, a Palladian design element that gave it more importance. The plan of the house, an "H" shape, is based on Elizabethan or Jacobean country houses. A protruding water table separates a lower level laid in Flemish bond from the upper or main level of lighter-colored brick. Doors at the ends of its halls and on either side of the Great Hall allow capture of any breezes during hot Tidewater summers. Though Stratford Hall was home to generations of Lees, it is interpreted today in four distinct periods of occupation. The house remains one of the most unique, striking and sophisticated of the extant mansions from early colonial Virginia.

ABOVE In the library there is a portrait of Revolutionary War
General Lafayette that he presented to Henry Lee. The painting
is attributed to Charles Peale Polk. A secretary desk like the one
exhibited here would have been used for correspondence and
conducting the general business of the plantation.

RIGHT The Federally detailed Chamber, located at the front
of the house at the end of the east passage, receives light and
ventilation from the south and east. Robert E. Lee was born
in this room in 1807.

ABOVE AND RIGHT *Among the outbuildings of the
plantation are a kitchen, a smokehouse, an overseer's
office, the gardener's and servants' houses, and a coach
house and stables. The north lawn stretches to the
Potomac River, where Philip Ludwell Lee had his
wharf, warehouse, and ship's store.*

MOUNT VERNON

Fairfax County, c. 1743 structure transformed by Lawrence Washington
who named it Mount Vernon;
1754 George Washington begins residency at Mount Vernon
and makes repairs; additions c.1757; additions 1775–1787
Owned and operated by the Mount Vernon Ladies' Association

PRECEDING PAGES *For more than forty years George Washington remodeled Mount Vernon, his estate on the Potomac River, transforming it from a small house with a central hall and two rooms on either side into one of the most beautiful country seats in America. The impression of his Palladian-inspired design is that of simple elegance. Arcaded hyphens, flanking the main house that connect it to dependency buildings create spaciousness and visually elongate the west entrance, giving it a more substantial presence.*

RIGHT *In 1787 Washington had the front parlor to the west painted Prussian blue. Its luxurious feeling comes from the profusion of ornately carved wood ornamentation. Elements include fully paneled walls, a classical pediment over the doorway, a mantel with a finely carved frieze and brackets, and a chimney breast elaborately carved in the rococo style. The room was used for small formal gatherings.*

*M*ount Vernon is the Washington family seat and long-time home of George Washington, the preeminent guiding force during America's formation. His unequalled leadership derived from the respect of his fellow statesmen for his strength of character, his skill and ability at unifying diverse interests, his courtly demeanor and commanding physical stature, and his upstanding goodness. He was and is America's seminal heroic figure.

Thousands of visitors have passed through Mount Vernon over the years, and beyond the capacity of the house as a welcoming destination, it was an office, a retreat, and a family residence. The Washingtons raised two sets of children here, neither progeny of George. The first consisted of Martha's two children by her former marriage to Daniel Parke Custis, and the second of grandchildren, the two youngest of Martha's son after he died as a young man.

From the time George Washington was twenty-two until his death in 1799, a focus of his mind and heart was his occupation as a farmer at his beloved Mount Vernon. His astute management of the estate, which he increased from 2,100 to 8,000 acres during his forty-five years in residence, involved changing his major crop of tobacco to wheat and other grains, raising livestock, breeding horses, and diversifying into fishing, milling, and later distilling businesses, leaving the estate debt-free at the time of his death. Today the Mount Vernon estate includes in its 500 acres not only the mansion and its dependencies, but fields, meadows, and mature woodlands, as well as Washington's landscape plans for the well-manicured lawns and formally designed vegetable, flower, and herb gardens.

The remodeling of Mount Vernon was a project that captured his creative mind. With a keen interest in architecture and an

extensive architectural library, Washington continually upgraded and enlarged the original four-room-and-hall plantation house into the mansion we see today. Although neither a trained architect nor designer, he nonetheless transformed the house into one of the most beautiful mansions in America. That it was never far from his thoughts is proven by his continual and detailed correspondence with various managers of the estate while he was away, either fighting the war, attending a Continental Congress or a U.S. Constitutional Convention, or serving as president. In successive phases he changed the appearance of the typical Virginia house into a Palladian-inspired country villa.

After 1757 Washington added a second story and new attic, and re-clad the west and east façades with wide wood siding that was chamfered, painted, and rusticated with sand to assimilate stone. Inside, he added cornice molding, chair rails, paneling, and built a handsome new walnut staircase. A window moved from under the staircase into

OPPOSITE TOP *The small parlor on the east side of the house has plaster walls and a simple chair rail. After 1797 when Washington returned from serving his terms as president, the room was used as a common parlor for enjoying music or taking tea.*

OPPOSITE BOTTOM *Washington created a more elegant entry when he installed a new walnut staircase in the central passage and new paneling and elaborate woodwork that included a cornice molding matching that of the exterior. The wood is finished with a faux bois technique. The key to the Bastille, a gift from the Marquis de Lafayette to the president, is displayed in a small glass cabinet.*

ABOVE *In his private study, Washington could escape the myriad visitors and the busy world around him. This is also where he corresponded daily with neighbors and friends. His library was remarkably diverse and well stocked. Though lacking a formal education, Washington had an innately curious mind and became extremely well informed on many subjects. Pictured here, the study contains such original Washington furnishings as the terrestrial globe on stand, the c. 1790 mahogany and oak, black-leather revolving chair, and the c. 1797 secretary and desk.*

ABOVE *The c. 1790-1798 engraving, The Washington Family, by Edward Savage and David Edwin, hangs above the mantel of the marble-sided fireplace in the small dining room, where the family took its smaller meals. The flourishes of rococo carving, the delicate design of the plasterwork ceiling, and the exciting verdigris paint color made this room extremely fashionable.*

RIGHT *The large formal dining room, a north wing addition, was begun by Washington in 1776. The elegantly proportioned room of 32 by 24 feet, which took more than eleven years to complete, was carefully directed by Washington in every detail of its design and construction through correspondence from afar. Of particular beauty are the tall Palladian-style window on the north wall that fills the room with light and the delicate decoration of the plaster ceiling. The elegant entertainment space accommodated large gatherings of friends, which the Washingtons loved to host.*

ABOVE *After the death of her husband, Martha Washington moved into a westerly facing garret chamber on the third floor. In this recently interpreted room, the original bedstead has bedhangings and a coverlet reproduced in cheery gold damask similar to that which Martha chose for her private space.*

RIGHT *A separate stairway and entrance to the Washingtons' second floor bedroom allowed privacy and separation from the rest of the house. The room is furnished with the bed in which Washington died, Martha's knee-hole dressing bureau, and a tray with one of Martha's porcelain tea services set for tea.*

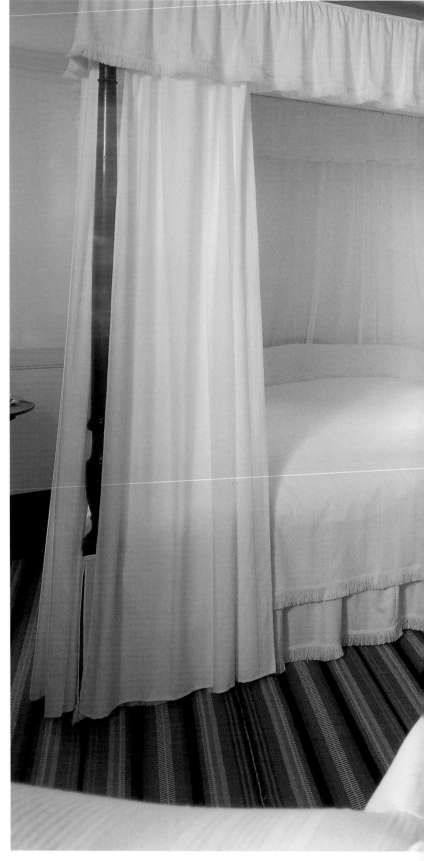

the adjacent room created asymmetry on the west front. In 1775 he had the small family dining room embellished with an ornately carved mantel and over mantel and a highly detailed decorative plaster ceiling. Beginning in 1773 he guided the addition of a south wing with the master bedroom and study and beginning in 1776 the addition of the 32-by-24-foot north dining room. Later, he added the piazza on the east façade and reconfigured and enlarged the flower and vegetable gardens. Through all of this construction, the result is a quiet and elegant statement of surprisingly human scale.

TOP *The well-designed proportion of the arcade and the rhythm of its carved wooden piers creates a pleasing transition between the mansion and the servants' hall dependency.*

ABOVE *The salt house and the gardener's house were among dependency buildings on the north lane located near the upper garden.*

RIGHT *Washington's design for the well-ordered landscaping of Mount Vernon included placement of a large vegetable garden, the "lower garden" toward the south of the mansion, to be in symmetry with gardens on the north side of the estate. The well-conceived garden, with plants espaliered against the brick retaining walls, produced an abundance of food. Washington had the octagonal necessary moved to decoratively anchor the corner of the garden.*

LEFT *The 14-foot deep piazza on the east elevation was constructed in 1777. Through the centuries, artists have depicted this iconic and stately view of Mount Vernon.*

BELOW *From the east piazza, the lawn and land-scaping continue to the banks of the Potomac River. The land beyond has been put into protective easement for the enjoyment of future generations.*

MOUNT AIRY

Richmond County, 1758
Owner-builder; John Tayloe II
Owned by Mrs. H. Gwynne Tayloe, Jr.

The construction of Mount Airy on the Northern Neck by Colonel John Tayloe II began almost ten years prior to its completion date of 1758. It is one of only a handful of historic houses and estates still owned and lived in by descendants of the original builder. The Tayloe family also still farms the land. The estate had already been in the Tayloe family for over a hundred years when they began building the mansion on land overlooking the Rappahannock River Valley. Tayloe was a British-educated, fourth-generation tobacco planter who used as his reference for the house's design architectural books available to colonial builders of the day. It appears that the south river façade is derived from Plate LVIII, "a design for a gentleman in Dorsetshire," in British architect James Gibbs's *Book of Architecture*, published in 1725, and the north front façade from Haddo House in Aberdeenshire, Scotland, designed by William Adam and featured in *Vitruvius Scoticus*, published in 1750.

ABOVE *The east façade of main house contains Palladian windows with different designs for each of their central arches.*

RIGHT *The two stone piers in the forecourt, and their elaborate stone ornaments, formalize the entrance.*

OPPOSITE TOP *A view from the northeast shows the north loggia of the great house, stone ramp walls containing the wide entry stairs, and the west dependency building connected by a hyphen containing a passageway.*

OPPOSITE BOTTOM *The recessed loggia on the north facade provides a spacious entry into the great hall.*

FOLLOWING PAGES *The great hall is a grand space, with large 9' 9" double doors at the north and south ends and a 14' 2" ceiling. Family portraits include original paintings by Allen Ramsey and Charles Willson Peale.*

Mount Airy's design is the Palladian concept of the ideal agrarian estate where an owner's large house is flanked by dependencies to create a symmetrical and pleasing design. Each building's height, width, and length as well as the relationship between the structures are based on proportions that create a harmonious scheme. The Palladian movement began in England in the 1710s and in the following years publication of English translations of Vitruvius and Palladio and a plethora of architectural pattern books had a widespread affect on architecture in both England and the colonies. Several wealthy English planters in Virginia who desired to live in the latest English fashion adopted Palladian principles for their permanent homes.

Mount Airy is one of the most beautiful and sophisticated of Palladian villa designs in America. The unusual dark and

ABOVE *In the dining room, at the west end of the house, eighteenth-century family portraits displayed on the walls include that hung above the mirror of David Lyde, half-brother to builder John Tayloe II. The dining table belonged to William Allen Carrington, great-grandfather of Mount Airy's present owner, Mrs. H. Gwynne Tayloe, Jr.*

OPPOSITE *The cornice of the mantel contains fragments of William Buckland's work with egg and dart, acanthus leaves, and wall of Troy designs. It was salvaged from the fire of 1844 that destroyed the original interiors of Mount Airy. The portrait over the mantel, painted by John Woolaston, is of Governor George Plater of Maryland, brother of Mrs. John Tayloe II. The room contains brass andirons that are original to the house, and elegant mid-eighteenth-century English silver, including a delicate cake basket and candlesticks.*

pebbled local stone quarried from the estate was used for the body of its buildings along with complementary pale sandstone quarried at nearby Aquia for the accents of the distinctive chiseled quoining at the building's corners and window and door surrounds.

Mount Airy is today a regal and elegantly proportioned country house that stands among pastoral and wooded acreage original to the estate. Its interiors were reinterpreted in the nineteenth century after the original interiors, the work of famed designer William Buckland, were destroyed in a fire in 1844. Buckland had just completed his work at Gunston Hall in 1759 and did various work for the Carter family, but

Buckland's chief patron during his twelve-year residency in the Northern Neck was Colonel Tayloe. After Buckland moved to Annapolis, he worked on the interiors of the Chase-Lloyd House for Tayloe's son-in-law Edward Lloyd IV.

With pride, Mount Airy's current owner, Mrs. H. Gwynne Tayloe, Jr., exerts a knowledgeable presence in this historic treasure in her keeping, and has actively farmed the acreage for more than forty years. Her dignified, gentle manner exudes legendary Virginia hospitality as she welcomes guests to her home, one of the most exciting architectural treasures, and the only one of its kind in scale and authenticity in America today.

ABOVE *The portraits above the sideboard, both painted by John Woolaston, are of Colonel John Tayloe II, builder of Mount Airy, and his wife Rebecca Plater Tayloe with daughter, Mary. The dinnerware brought over from China in 1825 is Nanking in a Rouge de Fer pattern.*

RIGHT *In the library, to the east of the great hall, the mantel cornice is crafted from a fragment of the interior woodwork designed by William Buckland. The beaten brass surrounding the fireplace, like that in the dining room, was done over a hundred years ago. To create the raised design, thin pieces of brass were placed over a mold and beaten.*

FOLLOWING PAGES *Pastoral beauty surrounds Mount Airy, still a working farm.*

*J*ohn Carlyle, though not well known today, was one of the most remarkable men of his era. Within seven short years of his 1741 arrival in Virginia at age twenty-one as the colonial agent for the English tobacco merchant Hicks & Co., the ambitious and resourceful young man had become financially successful and had married Sarah Fairfax, daughter of William Fairfax, who was land agent for his cousin Thomas, sixth Lord Fairfax. Carlyle's marriage also brought him a new brother-in-law, Lawrence Washington, older half-brother to George. With the backing of his powerful new family, Carlyle's opportunities for business ventures grew, as did his wealth, and he took his place as one of the most prominent men of the day. Carlyle preferred to work behind the scenes, but his contributions to Alexandria and his adopted country were significant. With astute managerial skills, uncommon business savvy, and a strong sense of duty he continuously worked for the public good from the time he helped co-found Alexandria in 1749 until his death in 1780.

At the outset of what escalated into the French and Indian War, Carlyle was the merchant who outfitted Major George Washington's 500-man regiment for its foray into the back-

ABOVE *Here, a detail of the desktop of Colonel Carlyle's study suggests how business was conducted by the eighteenth-century merchant*

RIGHT *The room opposite the large chamber on the main floor is interpreted as Colonel Carlyle's study. These two rooms were the Carlyle's private quarters, and the study especially would have been the colonel's personal domain. The room has been furnished with a Williamsburg desk and bookcase, not unlike those listed in the inventory for Belvoir, the nearby seat of the Fairfax family, Carlyle's in-laws.*

country of the Ohio frontier to negotiate with the French. When negotiations failed, King George III responded by sending General Edward Braddock and a force of 1600 British soldiers to Virginia. On April 3, 1755, Carlyle hosted General Braddock and five colonial governors at his house to discuss King George's plan for military victory against the French.

In 1752 Carlyle began construction of his residence, an impressive Georgian mansion designed for grandeur and efficiency. Carlyle's house was ambitious for its size and its construction material, sandstone from the quarry at Aquia, thirty miles south. It was set back from the street, formalized with a large front lawn that emphasized its height as well as the façade's unusual surface, the smoothly tooled stone. The house plan was typical of the mid-eighteenth century, a wide center hall with two rooms on either side, repeated on a second level. Dependency buildings that included offices, a kitchen, and a smokehouse, among others, sat on two of the

LEFT *The dining room was the largest and most important room in the Carlyle House. It was where the Carlyles entertained, and became the focal point of their social life, furnished to convey the family's status and wealth. It was in this room that on April 14, 1755, Major General Edward Braddock, Commander-in-Chief of His Majesty's Forces in North America, convened a meeting of five royal governors. Carlyle called this gathering "the Grandest Congress . . . ever known on the Continent."*

ABOVE *The most important bedroom in the house would have been the Chamber, the private room of Mr. and Mrs. Carlyle. A bedstead with matching bed and window curtains was purchased from Carlyle's brother-in-law at Belvoir; here, fine silk reproductions approximate the original luxurious chintz fabric. A portrait of his mother (Rachel Murray Carlyle), a double chest and a mahogany dressing table are also exhibited in the room.*

FOLLOWING PAGES *Although all evidence of Colonel John Carlyle's eighteenth-century gardens was obliterated in the mid-nineteenth century, the present recreated garden features carefully researched plant materials which would have been available to the colonel. The Carlyle House garden provides three-fourths of an acre of open green space in the center of Old Town Alexandria.*

most prime lots in the new town, one a waterfront property on the bluff above the Potomac River, the other facing the town square and market place.

The scale of Carlyle's house anticipated a large family, but sadly the envisioned dynasty was never to be as all of the Carlyle male children were to die young. John Carlyle's life is an important part of American history that would have been largely unknown were it not for a chance comment made by his family's descendants, Sir Fitzroy and Lady Maclean, while visiting Alexandria from Scotland in the 1970s. In their home was a cache of letters written by John to his brother George in England. These invaluable family documents reveal not only Carlyle's personal journey but also information about the times in which this extraordinary individual lived.

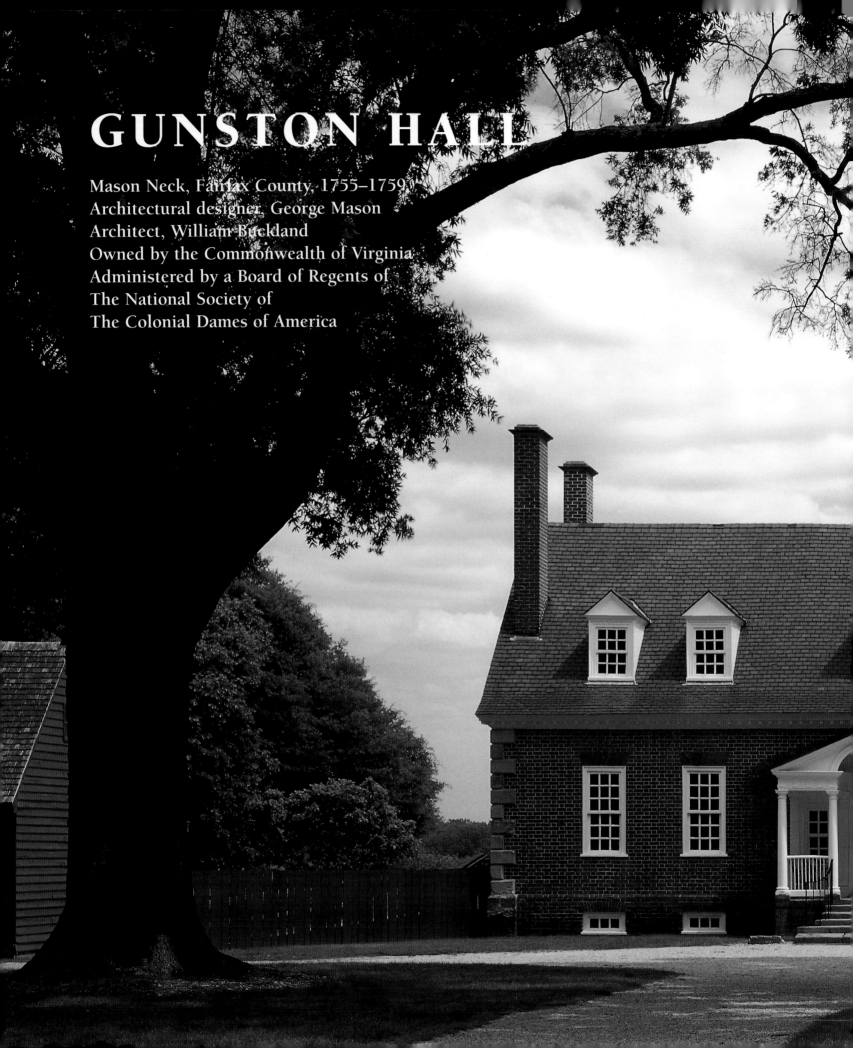

GUNSTON HALL

Mason Neck, Fairfax County, 1755–1759
Architectural designer, George Mason
Architect, William Buckland
Owned by the Commonwealth of Virginia
Administered by a Board of Regents of
The National Society of
The Colonial Dames of America

unston Hall was the residence of George Mason, a key figure in the formation of America's government. Neighbors and friends with whom he deliberated or corresponded included George Washington, Thomas Jefferson, James Madison, and John Marshall. Mason was respected for his intellectual prowess and fine reasoning skills, his unwavering character, his practical abilities, and his understanding of the history of law and government systems.

Mason was an extremely private man, who avoided political battles. He preferred the modest life of a plantation owner to a career in the large political arena, but when he felt public duty necessary, he served as a delegate in several important assemblies and conventions. His influence was instrumental in the formation of America's political system.

As a delegate to the Virginia Assembly in Williamsburg he was chiefly responsible for drafting the Virginia Declaration

OPPOSITE *The center passage was intended to impress visitors with its elaborately carved woodwork. Fluted pilasters, a frieze with triglyphs, a substantial cornice, two central arches, and a conspicuous pine-cone-shaped pendant between were all designed by William Buckland. The wallpaper is a reproduction of an English "pillar and arch" design originally printed in 1769.*

ABOVE *George Mason wrote many of his important documents in the little parlor, where the family often gathered for meals. The small desk in the foreground likely served as Mason's writing desk.*

of Rights. The document became the basis for the national Bill of Rights that Mason proposed, but was rejected, as part of the Constitution during the 1787 Continental Convention. Mason declined to sign the Constitution chiefly because it did not protect the individual's innate rights at a federal level. The Constitution was ratified by the states without this safeguard, but the new government soon adopted the Bill of Rights as its first ten amendments. Mason was vindicated.

Mason's plantation was called Gunston Hall after his family seat in England. The medium-sized house had a traditional Georgian plan of central hall and four rooms with a second story with seven bedchambers for a growing family. The handsome exterior was brick, fired on the property, and laid in Flemish bond pattern, with quoining at each corner cut from Aquia stone quarried nearby.

Construction was well underway by 1755 when talented twenty-two-year-old William Buckland, who had recently completed a seven-year apprenticeship in London as carpenter and joiner, arrived in Virginia. He had been recruited by Mason's brother, Thomson, to serve a four-year indenture to Mason. Buckland was to direct all construction on the house, as well as the interior design and woodwork. Buckland would become, in his short lifetime, a renowned architect. From his architectural books, he derived design motifs to create unique and spectacular interiors of complex, intricate carved-wood ornamentation. The primary carving was done

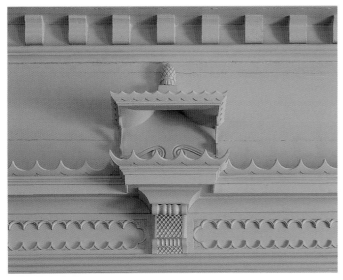

ABOVE *Hooded brackets above closet doorways and on the chimney breast were thought to have held decorative objects, probably Chinese export porcelain.*

RIGHT *The ornamental woodwork in the Chinese-inspired parlor confirms William Buckland's genius as a designer, and illustrates the superb carving skill of his assistant, William Bernard Sears. The meticulously proportioned decoration gives this public room its reputation as one of the most glorious in eighteenth-century Colonial, domestic architecture.*

FOLLOWING PAGES *The Palladian dining room, the most splendid room in the house, has an abundance of architectural ornamentation derived from the work of Renaissance architect Andrea Palladio. The impressive room's spectacular woodwork was unequalled in the colonies. Using his work at Gunston Hall as his calling card, Buckland went on to become a renowned designer and architect, with commissions in the Northern Neck of Virginia and Annapolis, Maryland.*

A one-acre garden includes Mason's original English boxwood allée and a broad lawn bordered by wide gravel paths. Further toward the Potomac River is a lower terrace level with flowers in boxwood parterres, overlooking a deer park studded by mature trees.

by Englishman William Bernard Sears. When completed in 1759, Gunston Hall contained the most exuberant explosion of visually captivating and beautiful interiors to be found in the colonies. It would become Buckland's calling card, leading to many commissions in Virginia's Northern Neck, his final work in Annapolis, and his legacy as one of the finest architects in colonial America.

Gunston Hall, intact and restored today, is a visible representation of the character of patriot and founding father George Mason: on the exterior, modesty, order, and strength; in the interior, a spectacular, complex, highly detailed beauty.

EYRE HALL

Northampton County, 1760;
addition prior to 1805 believed to incorporate a 1735 structure;
addition 1807
Owner-builder, Littleton Eyre
Owned by a direct descendent of Thomas Eyre I

$\mathcal{E}$yre Hall is a striking white weatherboard plantation house on Virginia's Eastern Shore that has evolved over time into a magnificent structure. The house appears, both inside and out, much as it did in the late eighteenth century. Its historical significance is conveyed through its original architecture, precious family heirloom furnishings, and continual ownership by the Eyre family. Today, its owner is a direct descendent of the original emigrant, Thomas Eyre I, who came to Jamestown in 1622 and arrived on the Eastern Shore in 1623. The current owner is the eighth continuous generation Eyre family member to live in the house and the eleventh generation on the Shore.

The original land from Thomas Eyre I was on the tip of the peninsula, a few miles south of Eyre Hall. In 1668, Governor Berkeley patented 1,600 acres to the three sons of Thomas I.

Littleton Eyre, great-grandson of Thomas Eyre I, purchased 700 acres in 1754 to build Eyre Hall. A dendrochronological analysis of the timbers in two of the three main sections of Eyre Hall indicated that the voluminous 41-foot-square wood frame two-and-a-half-story house was constructed in 1760. Attached to the east of this gambrel-roof house is a two-phased addition whose farthest section was built as a two-story unit in 1807; at the same time the intermediary section, circa 1790, was raised to two stories. Eyre Hall's modernization for contemporary living includes a spacious kitchen, breakfast room, and storage building built in the 1930s. The smokehouse was constructed from 1805 to 07 and a dairy built in 1760, with architectural detailing found only in one other such building (in Williamsburg), is the earliest known surviving dairy in Virginia. Four acres of flower and boxwood

PRECEDING PAGES *Eyre Hall, a magnificent eighteenth-century plantation house on the Eastern Shore, was constructed by Littleton Eyre, great-grandson of immigrant Thomas Eyre I who arrived on the Eastern Shore in 1623. The house, whose west section dates to 1760, is one of only a few still owned by descendents of the families who built them. Additions to the east of the 1760 structure date to 1790 and 1807.*

OPPOSITE TOP *The c. 1760 dairy is the earliest known surviving dairy in Virginia. Strigil ornamentation, the unusual design for ventilation found under the soffit, is named for its shape of the curve of a scraper.*

OPPOSITE BOTTOM *The c. 1760 western section of the house is a massive 41-foot square building with a gambrel roof. Each elevation has a separate entrance and wooden porch. Here, the porch on the south gives entry into the large front hall.*

ABOVE *Ruins of the c. 1819 neoclassical scored-stucco over brick-work orangery add charm to the rural estate. Directly to the north of the house, a four-acre garden includes a c. 1800 original boxwood garden, one of the oldest in America, specimen trees of the same period, and a profusion of flowering plants.*

gardens are surrounded by lawns and fields that glide into the salt marsh of Cherrystone Creek. The walled circa 1800 garden includes boxwood hedges from that period, the picturesque ruins of an unusual 1819 stucco and brick orangery, and a family cemetery.

The interior is particularly evocative of the era, with family furnishings purchased for the house from the late eighteenth to the early nineteenth centuries in rooms with original eighteenth century woodwork. A wide, crisply carved wood arch separates the elongated entry hall into two parlors, one ornamented with fully paneled walls and a substantial cornice at its twelve-foot ceiling. The other, with a door opening to the formal gardens, contains a paneled dado and above it, on the three walls, rare hand-blocked French wallpaper, circa 1815, by Dufour et Cie depicting exotic scenes

OPPOSITE *Many pieces of Baltimore painted furniture were originally purchased for the house. The unusual c. 1830 sixty-six key piano-organ was made by Nunns & Clark. Rare c. 1815 hand-blocked French wallpaper by Dufour et Cie dominates the room and gives it a lively atmosphere.*

ABOVE *A grandly scaled arch creates an intermediary space in the front hall, sometimes used for music and dancing. One of the finest pieces in the house is the c. 1750 Williamsburg gaming table placed under the arch. In the foreground the rare c. 1804 barrel organ, made in London, may be played to fill the room with evocative, carousel-style music that creates a powerful presence of the past.*

ABOVE *The grand scale and fine wood ornamentation of the formal parlor give it importance. The Adamesque mantel was added later, but the pilasters, which match those of the music room arch, are original. The portrait painted by Benjamin West positioned over the mantel is Severn Eyre, the son of builder Littleton Eyre. Above a c. 1820 Duncan Phyfe drop-leaf table is a portrait by Thomas Sully of Severn's son, John Eyre, who furnished the house in its lavish eighteenth- and early-nineteenth-century style.*

RIGHT *In the Federally styled formal dining room, priceless heirlooms include a set of Williamsburg chairs, as well as the Eyre family silver engraved with "L & B" for Littleton Eyre, the builder, and his wife Bridget, c. 1800 monogrammed Chinese export porcelain, and an English silver punch bowl made in 1692 that has always been in the Eyre family. The c. 1830 portrait is Sally Eyre Taylor painted by Thomas Sully.*

in "Les Rives de Bosphore." The interior throughout exudes sophistication in its spaciousness and fine ornamental wood-work. Family portraits by Benjamin West, Thomas Sully, and James Peale, a collection of fine English silver, crystal, and porcelain commissioned with a family monogram, original brasses, and furniture purchased in London or custom made in Baltimore or Williamsburg emphasize the Eyre family's legacy. The Eyre family motto *Si Je Puis* (If I Can) surely denotes the spirit of determination with which the family seat has been preserved.

ABOVE *Rare, ornate brasses on these doors in the private second floor quarters are all original to the home.*

RIGHT *In the library a black marble Federal mantel sets off the original heart pine paneling stripped of layers of paint in the 1930s. The portrait over the mantel is a copy by Thomas Sully of the Severn Eyre portrait by Benjamin West. Elsewhere in the room are framed seventeenth- and eighteenth-century maps showing the "Golden Quarter," the original land patent of the Eyre family.*

MONTICELLO

Albemarle County, 1769; remodel 1796–1809
Architect, Thomas Jefferson
Owned and operated by the Thomas Jefferson Foundation, Inc.

PRECEDING PAGES *Thomas Jefferson designed his home, Monticello, as the centerpiece of his 5,000-acre plantation located near Charlottesville. Over a period of forty years, from 1769 to 1809, he constructed and remodeled the house, significantly altering the design with neoclassical elements after 1796 and eventually enlarging it into a twenty-one room mansion.*

ABOVE AND RIGHT *Monticello, a National Historic Landmark and the only American site on the United Nations' World Heritage List, receives approximately 500,000 visitors annually. Since 1923 it has been owned and operated as a museum by the Thomas Jefferson Foundation, Inc.*

Thomas Jefferson, a singular figure in American history, was a Renaissance man possessed with formidable brilliance and a broad spectrum of talents and interests. In a life devoted to his state and country, Jefferson spent an exceptional amount of time in intellectual pursuit and the management of his plantation. One of his particular joys and great talents was his avocation as an architect. He consulted on plans for the houses of many of his friends and designed important public buildings including the Capitol in Richmond and the University of Virginia as well as his two residences—his retreat at Poplar Forest, in Bedford County, and Monticello. From 1768 to 1809, years during which he was indispensable to the founding of a country, Jefferson took delight in designing, modifying, constructing, and remodeling Monticello. It was where he lived until his death on July 4, 1826.

LEFT *In the entrance hall, a reception room for visitors, Jefferson created a cultural history museum with displays of classical and European art, maps of the vicinity and the known world, and skins, bones, and horns of living and extinct North American animals, in addition to some of the objects acquired by Lewis and Clark's exploring party from the indigenous tribes they encountered.*

ABOVE *The large parlor, the walls of which were filled with paintings, was used as the main entertainment space, where music, games, and conversation took place. The room looks out onto the west portico, lawn, and gardens.*

Jefferson's leadership included service in the House of Burgesses and in the Continental Congress, authorship of the Declaration of Independence, and terms as governor of Virginia, minister to France, secretary of state, and vice president and president of the United States. He is known as "The Sage of Monticello," a genius who knew seven languages and read works in their original texts, studied classical philosophy and political science, played violin quite well, gardened with a passion, maintained a vineyard, brought up a family including thirteen grandchildren, and who was willing to sacrifice his fortune, lands, home, and life for the sake of American independence.

In 1768 Jefferson began to level a building site on the little mountain that he had inherited from his father. The next year he would begin construction of a house that would change form over the next forty years. The first main house, essentially finished by 1779, was two stories with a loggia at the east entrance, over which there may have been a portico of Palladian design. Workshops and slave quarters were built along a nearby road that would become known as Mulberry Row.

LEFT AND ABOVE *The dining room and adjacent well-lit tea room are beautiful as well as functional. Outstanding architectural elements in the dining room are an elaborate classical-style frieze bordering the perimeter of the 17' 9"-high ceiling and graceful, wide arches. The tea room may be separated from the dining room by glass double partition doors. In these rooms Jefferson served sumptuous meals that included the bounty of his large vegetable garden and always the finest wine.*

ABOVE *Martha Jefferson Randolph, Jefferson's only surviving child, lived at Monticello with her large family during her father's retirement, serving as hostess and household manager. This small sitting room, adjacent to Jefferson's private study and living quarters, became Martha's office and the classroom where she taught her younger children.*

RIGHT *The parlor was filled with furnishings that served the different uses of the room. It was used for large, social, as well as small, informal family gatherings.*

Five years in Paris as minister to France from 1784 to 1789 confirmed Jefferson's love of European architecture and inspired him to rework Monticello's design. Remodeling from 1796 to 1809 entirely changed its look. It was enlarged to twenty-one rooms and transformed into a unique American design that showed influences of French and Roman as well as Palladian architecture. Features by 1809 included the L-shaped wings, flanking the main house, in which dependency rooms for slave quarters, the kitchen, the cellar, stables, and other facilities were built at a basement level. A terrace walkway level with the flooring of the house was built on their roofs. The phased construction also included roads encircling the mountain from its base to the top, a pavilion at the north terminal end of the dependency wing that mirrored a south pavilion built circa 1770, a large vegetable garden, and an orchard. The fascinating house, now on the World Heritage List, truly reflects its builder, a complicated combination of public figure and private citizen, unlike any other man of his time.

OPPOSITE *Jefferson's private apartment contained his bed-chamber, a cabinet or study, a library, and a greenhouse. Through the arch leading from his library, the contents of which became the core of the U.S. Library of Congress, we see the furnishings in his cabinet that include his writing table, chair, and bench for resting his legs, a portable revolving bookstand, and a polygraph machine. In these private rooms Jefferson could retreat from the business of the plantation to contemplate and read.*

TOP *The dome room, on the third floor, is an architectural delight, simple and pure in its form. In Jefferson's time it may have been used as extra sleeping quarters or for storage.*

ABOVE *Jefferson's cabinet and double-height bedroom are separated by his bed alcove which has a storage area for clothes overhead. The bedroom contains a skylight. The suite of rooms was designed for privacy, efficiency, and beauty. A glass-enclosed greenhouse is accessible from the library.*

RIGHT *The two-acre vegetable garden on the southeast slope of the mountain served as a laboratory for Jefferson's horticultural interests and yielded a bounty of produce served in the dining room. In 1809 the garden was 1,000 feet long by 80 feet wide. There was an orchard below it and Mulberry Row, the main street of the plantation, on the ridge above.*

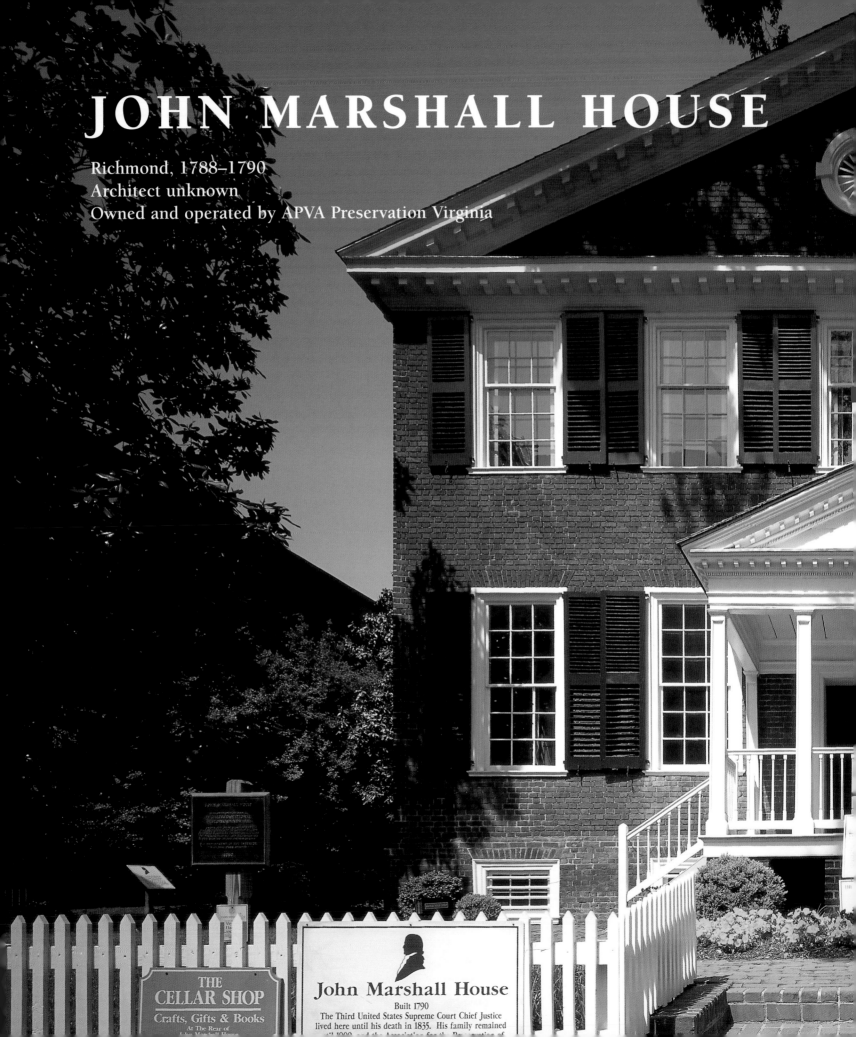

JOHN MARSHALL HOUSE

Richmond, 1788–1790
Architect unknown
Owned and operated by APVA Preservation Virginia

THE
CELLAR SHOP
Crafts, Gifts & Books
At The Rear of
John Marshall House

John Marshall House
Built 1790
The Third United States Supreme Court Chief Justice
lived here until his death in 1835. His family remained

John Marshall House

OPEN

Tuesday-Saturday   Sunday

PRECEDING PAGES *The John Marshall House, completed c. 1790, is owned and operated by APVA Preservation Virginia. It was the home of Chief Justice John Marshall and his family for more than forty years. The handsome Federal-style house was located in Court End, a fashionable residential neighborhood near the Capitol, and once stood in a complex of dependency buildings that covered four lots in the heart of Richmond.*

RIGHT *The withdrawing room, a small parlor at the back of the house, was used by the family for intimate informal gatherings as well as for formal entertaining. The fine woodwork includes floor to ceiling paneling. Flanking the classically styled mantel are a built-in cupboard with shelving for books and an arched entry, a c. 1810 addition to the room, leading into the house's central passage.*

FOLLOWING PAGES *The large room at the front of the house, with fine neoclassical wood ornamentation, was a multi-purpose space. Marshall used the room as a dining room for such lively dinners as those he hosted regularly for his law colleagues and friends, and as a parlor when entertaining Richmond society. Marshall's large mahogany library bookcase now furnishes the room, which also served as his office for a short while.*

*J*ohn Marshall, America's third chief justice of the Supreme Court, settled in Richmond as it was beginning to grow as a city. In 1780 Governor Thomas Jefferson moved the capital from Williamsburg to Richmond and laid out a fashionable neighborhood called Court End convenient to Capitol Square where a neoclassical courthouse was to be built. Newly married, Marshall moved to Richmond in 1783 to establish a law practice. Construction of his residence began in 1788 and when completed in 1790 was an urban estate that included a Federal-style brick dwelling house and dependency buildings on a full city block in Court End. It was to be the Marshall home for forty-five years at the core of the capital city's political and social activity. Here he and his wife Mary Willis Ambler (known in the family as Polly) raised a family of six, provided jovial evenings once a month for fellow lawyers and statesmen, hosted dignitaries, and centered a life of public service.

With an education limited to instruction by his father during childhood on Virginia's frontier, two years of private tutoring by clergymen, and a brief study of law at the College of William and Mary in Williamsburg, it is astounding that at the age of eighteen John Marshall passed the bar and was poised for a legal career. However, in 1775 at age twenty he began service in the Revolutionary War, first in the Culpeper Minutemen and later in other Virginia regiments. He became

ABOVE *The Marshalls' master bedchamber is a large room in the private quarters upstairs. Marshall heirlooms found in the house include the c. 1800 needlepoint-upholstered wing chair, a shaving kit, and a c. 1770 sampler made by Mary Ambler (Mrs. Marshall), seen here.*

OPPOSITE TOP *The north bedchamber on the upper floor probably served as a guest room after the Marshall's children left home. The room's furnishings include the c. 1810 high post bed, a damask-upholstered wing chair, a tea table and tea service, and a writing desk.*

OPPOSITE BOTTOM *The French ebony-veneer mantel clock was purchased by the Marshalls in 1810. Marshall acquired a taste for the refined style of French decorative arts and architecture during his year in Paris as an envoy sent by President John Adams to negotiate a trade agreement with French Foreign Minister Tallyrand in what was to become known as the "XYZ affair."*

a captain in the Continental Army and was George Washington's Deputy Judge Advocate at Valley Forge. His mentorship by Washington and military hardships engrained in him a passionate belief for a strong central government that he would carry into his later life and would crystallize as he grew into the first and chief interpreter of the U.S. Constitution.

While living in Richmond, Marshall balanced the demands of a successful law practice with his popularity as a statesman, serving four terms as a member of the Virginia House of Delegates. But he gained national notoriety in 1798 when upon his return as an envoy to France his journal describing the shocking behavior of Minister Talleyrand and the failed reconciliation between the two nations was published. In subsequent years his desire to maintain a private

law practice would succumb to an ever-increasing sense of duty to serve his country. He was elected to the U.S. House of Representatives in 1799, named secretary of state in 1800 under President John Adams, and in 1801 became chief justice of the Supreme Court.

Marshall was a charismatic, natural leader whose intellectual brilliance, equaled by his convivial, even-tempered manner, his upstanding character and extraordinary integrity, and his astute linguistic clarity allowed him to pursue his unswerving dedication to a unified nation and the transformation of the Supreme Court from a weak entity into the core of a judicial branch whose power balances that of the executive and legislative branches. The legacy of his leadership of the Court for thirty-four years is the structure of our democracy and the source of our freedom.

GLEN BURNIE

Winchester, Frederick County, 1794; addition 1797;
additions nineteenth century; remodel 1955
Owner-builder, Robert Wood
Owner-renovator, Julian Wood Glass, Jr.
Owned by the Glass-Glen Burnie Foundation

The drawing room, which Mr. Glass created on the site of a former south wing using some of the bricks from that structure, contains a floor which has been lowered to increase the height of the room. An 18 by 38-foot custom-made reproduction of an eighteenth-century English Axminster rug covers the floor. Outstanding antique furnishings and artwork include a c. 1760–1770 mahogany Chippendale-style sofa with rolled arms and camel back and the c. 1850 portrait of George Washington by Rembrant Peale.

Winchester, Wood was a prominent citizen, serving as clerk of court, a position from which he recorded deeds and wills and generally had his finger on the pulse of the community's business.

When young George Washington came to Frederick County as surveyor for Lord Fairfax he very likely became acquainted with James Wood. Through the years 1746 to 1758 Washington's ties to Frederick County became strong and complex as he resided there intermittently. He constructed Fort Loudoun in Winchester as his regimental headquarters during the French and Indian War. His ownership of land qualified him to run for elected office, and though Washington's first attempt failed, with the help of James Wood, Washington won a seat in the House of Burgesses in 1758 for the first of two terms. In 1797 James Wood's granddaughter Mary Dorcas married Washington's nephew Lawrence Augustine Washington.

Later, Winchester's location at the junction of nine major roads and a railway line caused it to be a strategic site in the Civil War, the scene of encampments, battles, and early headquarters for General Stonewall Jackson.

James Wood's original house no longer exists. The Glen Burnie we see today began as a two-story, one-room-deep

ABOVE *The breakfast room in the north wing of the house was built by Julian Wood Glass, Jr., with a doorway to connect it to the older main house. The cupboards are filled with numerous sets of dinnerware, including a 1745 set of white embossed Meissen. In the center of the room a c. 1808 Sheffield silver candelabra sits on a c. 1740–1760 mahogany Queen Anne drop leaf table.*

RIGHT *The dining room today was the parlor of the 1797 addition, built by Robert Wood. The three-part walnut Hepplewhite dining table is original to the house, as are the room's molding and floor. The rare carved Chippendale-style stepback cupboard is cherry.*

FOLLOWING PAGES *The warmth and luxuriousness of the library are due to the warm-toned paneling, mantel, and bookcases that were crafted from pine floorboards reclaimed from the attic. The room is part of the small original house, and served as the dining room and central room of the household. Antique furnishings and family heirlooms include a pair of American c. 1773 silver beakers made for James Wood, Jr. that rest on the mantel, an English brass chandelier c. 1790, and a c. 1800 Sheraton mahogany barrelback easy chair.*

ABOVE AND RIGHT *A set of stone columns with Ionic capitals frames a view of the rural countryside. A pleached allée leads to the small Palladian-style pavilion, with its brick courtyard and fountain.*

brick house built by James Wood's married son Robert in 1794. It was enlarged by 1797 into a two-story structure with a center hall with rooms on either side. Later additions to the house included north and south wings. In 1885 the house, through inheritance, came into the Glass family.

Beginning in 1956, Julian Wood Glass, Jr., the property's last private owner, improved it by dismantling the structurally unsound wings and rebuilding them using some of the original bricks. Over the next four decades he and Mr. R. Lee Taylor landscaped six acres with ornamental rose gardens, Chinese and water gardens, boxwood parterres and knot gardens, and a pleached allée of flowering crab apples.

Today his Glass-Glen Burnie Foundation enables the public to enjoy the house and gardens as well as a new regional history museum, the Museum of the Shenandoah Valley, among 250 acres of the original Wood land grant, an oasis within the thriving historic town.

CARTER HALL

Millwood, Clarke County, c. 1798; additions c. 1908; restoration and remodel 1930s
Owner -builder Nathaniel Burwell
Restoration Architect, Harry T. Lindeberg
Owned and operated by Project HOPE/The People to People Health Foundation, Inc.

PECEDING PAGES *Carter Hall, in Millwood, was constructed between 1792 and 1798 by Nathaniel Burwell, who had grown up at Carter's Grove near Williamsburg. The restored house is the centerpiece of a 200-acre estate owned and operated as their international headquarters by Project HOPE/The People to People Health Foundation, Inc.*

ABOVE AND RIGHT *Carter Hall is built of local limestone. Original dependency buildings that included a kitchen, stables, a barn, and a schoolhouse have been transformed into guest quarters for the Carter Hall Conference Center.*

*I*nspired and serendipitous timing in 1977 brought together Carter Hall, a historic house and estate then in need of a new owner and caretaker, and the international health organization Project HOPE (Health Opportunities for People Everywhere). Because its floating hospital S.S. HOPE had recently been retired, it was looking for a land base from which to administer the many-faceted health programs that it runs in over 30 countries worldwide. Project HOPE's global impact, in its permanent programs as well as its humanitarian aid to disaster areas, is unprecedented. Due to the change in its headquarters' location and sound financial management, on the average, an astonishing 92 percent of its multi-million dollar budget is allocated to its programs annually.

Carter Hall began as the centerpiece of one of the largest plantations in the Shenandoah Valley. Additional acreage was purchased to bring the total to 8,000 acres shortly after the house was constructed in about 1798 by owner Nathaniel Burwell. He had moved from his father's plantation, Carter's Grove near Williamsburg, to settle on his own lands and

PRECEDING PAGES *The commodious living room has been restored to Georgian elegance with classically styled ornamental woodwork and a sweeping staircase that leads to guestrooms on the second floor. The two-year, multimillion-dollar restoration was completed in the 1930s for then-owner Gerard B. Lambert by noted New York architect Harry T. Lindeberg.*

ABOVE *The formal dining room, located to the west of the living room, is furnished with a large dining table that may be expanded to seat eighteen. The room's elegant woodwork includes fully paneled walls, a classically styled cornice, and a mantel flanked by carved pilasters.*

OPPOSITE *The sitting room located east of the living room has elaborately carved pediments over each doorway. Thirteen-foot ceilings in the public rooms on the first floor create elegance and spaciousness.*

FOLLOWING PAGES *Fine architectural detailing in the pine-paneled library includes built-in bookcases and tall sash windows. An equestrian scene over the mantel is a historical reference to fox hunting and thoroughbred breeding, two endeavors enjoyed by centuries of Carter Hall owners.*

From the south-facing front porch with its huge columns, an addition completed around 1830, a view of the landscaped 200-acre estate evokes an idyllic past.

establish the village of Millwood. Built of limestone found on the property, the mansion was originally designed as a modest two-story house flanked by two large dependency buildings, a kitchen and a schoolhouse, to create the symmetry of a Georgian estate. Other service buildings included a smoke house and stables.

Descendents of the Burwell family lived in and protected Carter Hall through the Civil War, though by 1865 the mansion and grounds were in poor condition. Throughout the war, the village of Millwood and its surrounding estates, many of which were owned by Burwell cousins and extended family members, saw continual and heavy traffic of both Union and Confederate troops, including those of General

Robert E. Lee, Stonewall Jackson, Jeb Stuart, and local hero, Captain John Singleton Mosby.

Carter Hall changed hands several times and experienced alterations. In the 1930s the mansion was purchased by Gerard B. Lambert, who had made his fortune before the stock market crash by turning Listerine, a surgical antiseptic developed by his father, into America's most famous mouthwash. Lambert hired noted New York architect Harry T. Lindeberg for a two-year, multi-million dollar remodel that would restore the mansion to its former glory by removing various inappropriate nineteenth- and early-twentieth-century "modernizations." They upgraded the roofs and gutters, replaced the current non-historic stair-case with a graceful flying staircase in the great room, and added a front porch with monolithic Ionic columns to give the house the air of a country manor. Lambert's improvements were honored and the estate beautifully maintained by subsequent owners.

How fortunate that Carter Hall was purchased by Project HOPE, which should be thanked not only for its impact on millions of the world's most needy citizens through implementation of programs of long term health education and training, primary health care, and disaster relief, but also for its role as historic preservationist, maintaining and sharing the loveliness of Carter Hall as a conference center amidst the park-like 200 acres that form the estate today.

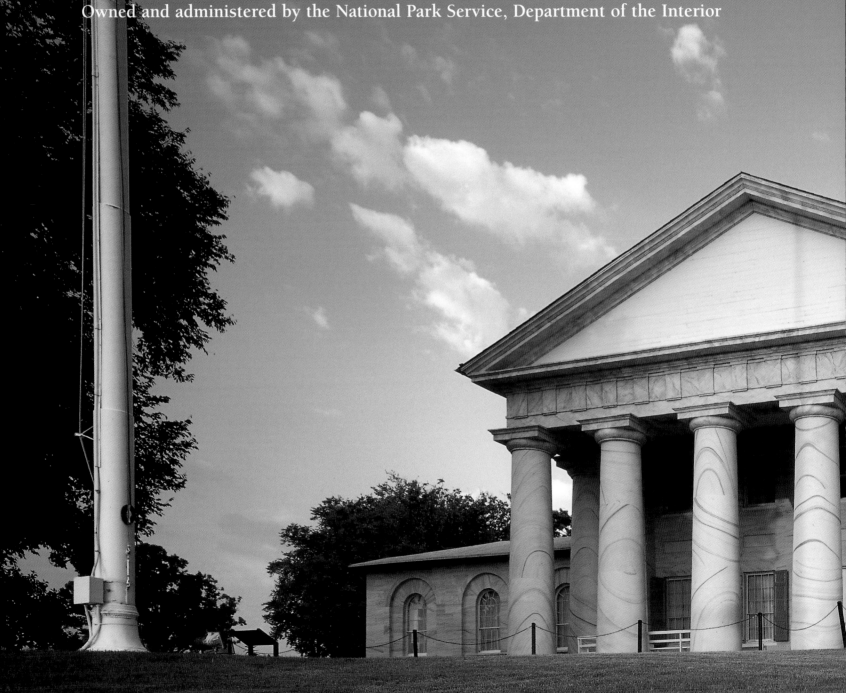

ARLINGTON HOUSE

The Robert E. Lee Memorial
Arlington County, c. 1802–1818
Architect, George Hadfield
Owned and administered by the National Park Service, Department of the Interior

PRECEDING PAGES *Arlington House, The Robert E. Lee Memorial, was built in three phases from 1802 to 1818 by George Washington Parke Custis, George Washington's step-grandson. The most striking feature of the two-story plantation house is the east portico, with its monolithic columns. The house sits on a bluff overlooking the Potomac River and Washington, D.C. in what is now Arlington National Cemetery. It is owned and maintained by the National Park Service, U.S. Department of the Interior.*

ABOVE *The center hall affords a most stunning view of the river and city below. On its walls are family portraits that include copies of Charles Willson Peale's portrait of George Washington and John Wollaston's portrait of Martha Washington, both owned by Robert E. Lee. A copy of the portrait of Washington at Yorktown was painted by George Washington Parke Custis.*

RIGHT *The morning room was also the painting studio of George Washington Parke Custis, a gentleman of diverse interests who wrote plays, poetry, and speeches that promoted the glorification of the nation's most important hero, George Washington. His American Revolutionary War scenes included the Battle of Monmouth, New Jersey, displayed here.*

rlington House, once known as the Custis Lee Mansion, sits on a high bluff overlooking Washington, D.C., the Potomac River, and Arlington Cemetery. It is the national memorial to General Robert E. Lee, who, after the Civil War, served as President of Washington College (now Washington and Lee University in Lexington, Virginia), and helped, as no other American could have, to bring about peace and reconciliation in the nation. His strong character and integrity ennobled him to his countrymen then, and to future generations of Americans.

ABOVE AND LEFT *The white parlor, finished by the Lees in 1855, contains their Victorian parlor furniture, including crimson velvet-upholstered settees and side chairs. The marble mantels were the choice of Robert E. Lee. Copies of portraits of Robert E. Lee as a young army lieutenant and his wife Mary Custis hang above the mantels.*

Ironically, the mansion, built in three phases from 1802 to 1818, was originally meant to be a monument to another great American, George Washington. It was conceived by George Washington Parke Custis, the grandson of Martha Washington who was raised by the Washingtons at Mount Vernon after the death of his father, who had purchased the 1,100 acres in 1778 as his future family seat. Custis inherited the land when he reached his age of majority in 1802.

Custis first called the estate Mount Washington, building it as a national shrine to his adored guardian. Custis inherited various personal items after the deaths of George and Martha Washington, and purchased many others at great cost. The memorabilia were displayed for public admiration at the Mount Washington museum.

Custis was one of the most active and successful early promoters of American culture. From Washington's example and

ABOVE *It is believed that Robert E. Lee proposed to his distant cousin Mary Custis in this family dining room. Original Lee furnishings include the twin serving tables and Mount Vernon knife boxes, pieces of china, and silver that includes an American tea kitchen engraved with the Lee coat of arms. Triple arches lead to the family parlor.*

RIGHT *Lieutenant Robert E. Lee and Mary Custis were married in the family parlor, a large room that faces the front of the house. Its silk-upholstered furnishings are those purchased by the Custises in about 1825. The c. 1831 portrait of Mary Anna Randolph Custis that hangs above the mantel was painted by Auguste Hervieu.*

teaching he had become a gentleman of diverse interests and accomplishments. Custis was passionately nationalistic about people recognizing themselves as Americans. This led him to write dramas for the theatre, deliver speeches, recite his own poetry, paint large-scale war scenes from the American Revolution, and above all, to create and maintain the museum to glorify the nation's most important hero, George Washington.

During his years at Arlington House, as Custis had renamed it in 1804, he and his wife Molly Fitzhugh's only surviving child, Mary Anna Randolph Custis, grew up playing with the children of her parents' friends who lived nearby. In 1831 she married her childhood friend and distant cousin, Robert E. Lee. During the early years of their marriage they lived between Arlington House and the various forts

ABOVE *The George Washington Parke Custis bedchamber is where both he and his wife died. It is in the oldest section of the house, the north wing, and contains the original mantel.*

RIGHT *In the Lees' bedchamber on the second floor, Robert E. Lee wrote his momentous resignation from the United States Army on April 20, 1861. Two days later he left Arlington House, and his wife and family moved out within a month, never to return to their home.*

where Lee's career in the U.S. Army took him and raised seven children.

At the onset of the Civil War, on April 20, 1861, after having been offered command of the Union forces, Robert E. Lee resigned his U.S. Army post, after a distinguished career of 32 years. From Arlington House he wrote the letter of resignation, knowing that by doing so he would be sacrificing his career, his home, and possibly his life. On April 23, he accepted command of the Army of Northern Virginia. He and his family left Arlington House in 1861, never to return.

After the war, General Lee spoke persuasively for reuniting the country, for partisan interests to bury the past and reconcile their differences for the sake of the nation. In 1925 Congress established this house as a memorial to honor Robert E. Lee and restoration to its 1861 condition began in 1928. Since 1933, Arlington House, The Robert E. Lee Memorial has been owned and operated by the National Park Service.

OATLANDS

Loudoun County, 1804; additions 1820s; additions 1830s
Owner-builder, George Carter
Owned in co-stewardship by the National Trust for
Historic Preservation and Oatlands, Inc.

The Northern Virginia mansion of Oatlands has weathered vicissitudes from its creation as the centerpiece of a thriving plantation, through wartime and subsequent use as a girls school and boarding house, to its current status as a museum house owned by the National Trust for Historic Preservation and maintained by Oatlands, Inc.

The 3,400 acres on which Oatlands was constructed were part of a 63,000-acre tract purchased in 1776 by Robert Carter III, known as the "Councillor." As an act of conscience this remarkable man, by his daring, complex, and controversial Deed of Gift, began in 1791 the gradual and systematic emancipation of over 500 slaves on his twenty plantations. By the time of the Councillor's death in 1804 he and his agent Benjamin Dawson had freed 260 slaves. Dawson worked on into 1826 and even as late as 1852 Carter's 69-year-old daughter Julia was still freeing descendants of her father's slaves.

PRECEDING PAGES Oatlands was begun in 1804 by George Carter and was the centerpiece of a 3,400-acre plantation. The house became a definitive Greek Revival-style structure when the front portico was added in 1827. Today the National Historic Landmark is owned in co-stewardship by the National Trust for Historic Preservation and Oatlands, Inc.

OPPOSITE AND ABOVE In the spacious entry foyer spectacular ornamentation includes a plaster ceiling medallion, elaborately carved woodwork such as this blind arch above a doorway, and a heavily detailed plaster cornice. Full-length portraits show Mr. Eustis's parents, Louise Corcoran Eustis and George Eustis, painted during their honeymoon in Rome in 1859.

FOLLOWING PAGES The original fireplace surround in the dining room includes an ornate mantel carved with Adam-style ornamentation flanked by pilasters that match the front portico columns. The mahogany sideboard and knife boxes, attributed to John Needles of Baltimore, Maryland, were purchased for the house in 1824 by George Carter. Family portraits hang on the walls.

In 1796 George Carter, the Councillor's youngest son, acquired 5,000 acres in Loudoun County by a lottery set up by his father to divide his holdings evenly among his ten surviving children. In 1804, Carter began construction of a mansion on a portion of this property using bricks fired on the property and stabilizing it on a rock base with gigantic oak beams of mortise and tenon joinery. Various changes were made to the house as Carter acquired funds to do so. The mansion became a definitive Greek Revival-style structure when the front portico was added in 1827. Two-story-tall columns with carved Corinthian capitals enhanced the grandeur of the entrance as did resurfacing the exterior walls with a buff-color paint over stucco made of sand, horsehair, and crushed limestone. Carter enlarged the house in 1828 by replacing a narrow interior staircase with a larger staircase enclosed in a wing to the east side, and in 1830 added a matching wing to the west. He also dec-

OPPOSITE *In the library a comfortable seating arrangement faces the beautiful early-nineteenth-century black marble mantel. The mahogany bookcases were added by the Eustises, converting this first-floor bedroom into a family room and reading area. Above the mantel is a portrait of Mr. Eustis's grandfather, W. W. Corocran. To the left is a portrait of Levi P. Morton, Mrs. Eustis's father.*

ABOVE *In the octagonal drawing room, elegantly furnished with a gold-gilt Louis XV settee and fauteuils, a portrait of Mrs. Eustis, painted by French artist Carolus Duran, may be seen in the reflection of the mirror over the mantel.*

ABOVE *The large bank barn, dug out from the side of a hill near the estate's lower eastern pasture, was once an integral part of the farming enterprise. The two-story building housed farm animals, grain storage, and farm equipment, and was the main focus of George Carter's working yard in the early to mid-nineteenth century.*

RIGHT *Of Oatlands' current 369 acres, four and a half are magnificent formal gardens restored by Mrs. William Corcoran Eustis after she and her husband purchased the estate in 1903.*

orated the interiors with finely carved wood and plaster ornamentation in the Adamesque and Greek Revival styles. By the time of his marriage at age 59 in 1836, Carter's self-sufficient plantation included a commercial grist mill at the center of a small village.

After Carter's death, his widow and two sons lived at Oatlands until the Civil War threatened the property. After the war, George Carter II and his wife Katherine reinvented Oatlands as a girls school and later a boarding house. Prestigious guests included Phoebe Hearst, the wealthy San Francisco socialite and mother of William Randolph Hearst.

In 1897 Oatlands was sold out of the Carter family, and was resold in 1903. The new owners, Mr. and Mrs. William Corcoran Eustis, had both the means and motivation to rejuvenate the historic estate. Mrs. Eustis, a passionate gardener, restored the original four-and-a-half acres of formal gardens and incorporated them into a larger more informal English country-style landscape. In 1965 the Eustises' two daughters donated Oatlands and the 261 acres on which it sits to the National Trust for Historic Preservation.

LONG BRANCH

Millwood, Clarke County, 1810–1818; design modifications, 1811;
additions, 1842
Architect, Benjamin Henry Latrobe (1811 design modifications)
Architect, Minard Lefever (1842 additions)
Owned and operated by The Harry Z. Isaacs Foundation

The history of Long Branch weaves together the stories of three of early Virginia's prominent families, the Carters, the Burwells, and the Nelsons, with that of a twentieth century owner, Harry Z. Isaacs. The latter returned the deteriorating early nineteenth-century country manor house to a state of elegant beauty, and with his gift of The Harry Z. Isaacs Foundation, has allowed for its preservation as an important part of the history of early Virginia for future generations.

In 1798 Robert Carter Burwell inherited 1,000 acres in Virginia's bucolic Shenandoah Valley. When he came of age in 1810 Burwell began construction of his home above the property's water source, a spring and creek known as Long Branch. The architectural design of the impressive brick mansion was refined with input from Benjamin Henry Latrobe, the preeminent architect in America of the day. Latrobe's suggestions as to how to give the house a better functioning and more livable interior space were adhered to as much as possible after they arrived by mail in 1811 after the brick foundations had been laid.

RIGHT *As part of Harry Z. Isaac's multimillion-dollar renovation and remodel of Long Branch, the west wing was added after 1986. The hunt room, so named for its French wallpaper of a hunt scene, is located adjacent to the entry hall and is furnished with fine antiques that include the c. 1800 cherry tallcase clock from Maryland. The French wallpaper, an eighteenth-century design produced by Zuber, is hand painted.*

FOLLOWING PAGES *The design of the spectacular Greek Revival woodwork in the two parlors on the main floor was added by Hugh Nelson in 1842 to give the interior Georgian elegance. The woodwork was meticulously restored with the removal of seventeen coats of paint, during the comprehensive restoration and remodel by Harry Z. Isaacs in the late 1980s.*

Burwell died in 1813 and the first phase of Long Branch's construction may have continued until 1818. By 1820 Long Branch had been legally inherited by his older sister Sarah and her husband Philip Nelson, who had been guardians of Burwell. They had moved to the area to supervise construction of great uncle Nathaniel Burwell's mill and to set up a mercantile operation in Millwood and later had bought property adjacent to young Burwell's, run in conjunction with his as a lucrative wheat farm. Nathaniel Burwell, great uncle of Robert Carter Burwell, lived at his nearby 5,000-acre-plantation Carter Hall. The Nelsons and their nine sons and daughters managed the wheat farm as their main source of income until the late 1820s. By 1831 Long Branch housed a girls school run by Nelson's daughters.

In 1842 Long Branch was purchased by Hugh Mortimer Nelson, Philip Nelson's nephew. He and his family undertook renovations and expansions that greatly altered the look of the large country manor. They created a battlement of the east service wing by enclosing the crenellated loggia and significantly altered the north and south façades by adding Greek Revival porticos. Throughout the interior, extensive carved woodwork created a Georgian elegance that was enhanced by a sweeping spiral staircase in the entry foyer

A failed wheat crop in 1857 brought Long Branch into great debt, and Nelson died a few years thereafter. Through the hardship of the Civil War and the general destruction of the Shenandoah Valley, the women at Long Branch endured and the structure survived unscathed. The estate would stay in Nelson hands until sold in 1957.

The house and grounds changed hands three times before Harry Z. Isaacs, a Baltimore textile manufacturer and successful horse breeder, drawn to the estate's history and its potential for restoration and refurbishment, bought it at auction in late 1986. Over the next three years Isaacs devoted his tremendous energy and wealth to reestablishing the grandeur of Long Branch and after the work was completed, put the historic estate into trust for future generations to enjoy. Today the 400-acre working farm and museum house are open to the public.

OPPOSITE *The elegant formal dining room is one of the spaces created from enclosure of the original loggia on the east wing of the house in 1842. Mr. Isaacs lavishly furnished the room with the fines antiques, such as the eighteenth-century knife boxes of American poplar, four large sterling silver candelabra, and works of equestrian art such as that painted by Richard Barrett Davis in the late nineteenth century.*

ABOVE *In the parlor, exquisite antiques include a small c. 1720 English bench with its original needlework, drawn up to the rare c. 1710 spinet piano.*

FOLLOWING PAGES *The 400-acre working farm and museum house of Long Branch are protected and maintained by The Harry Z. Isaacs Foundation. The estate, host to festivals and events throughout the year, is nestled within the rural splendor of the hills and valleys of Clarke County with unequalled views of the Blue Ridge Mountains.*

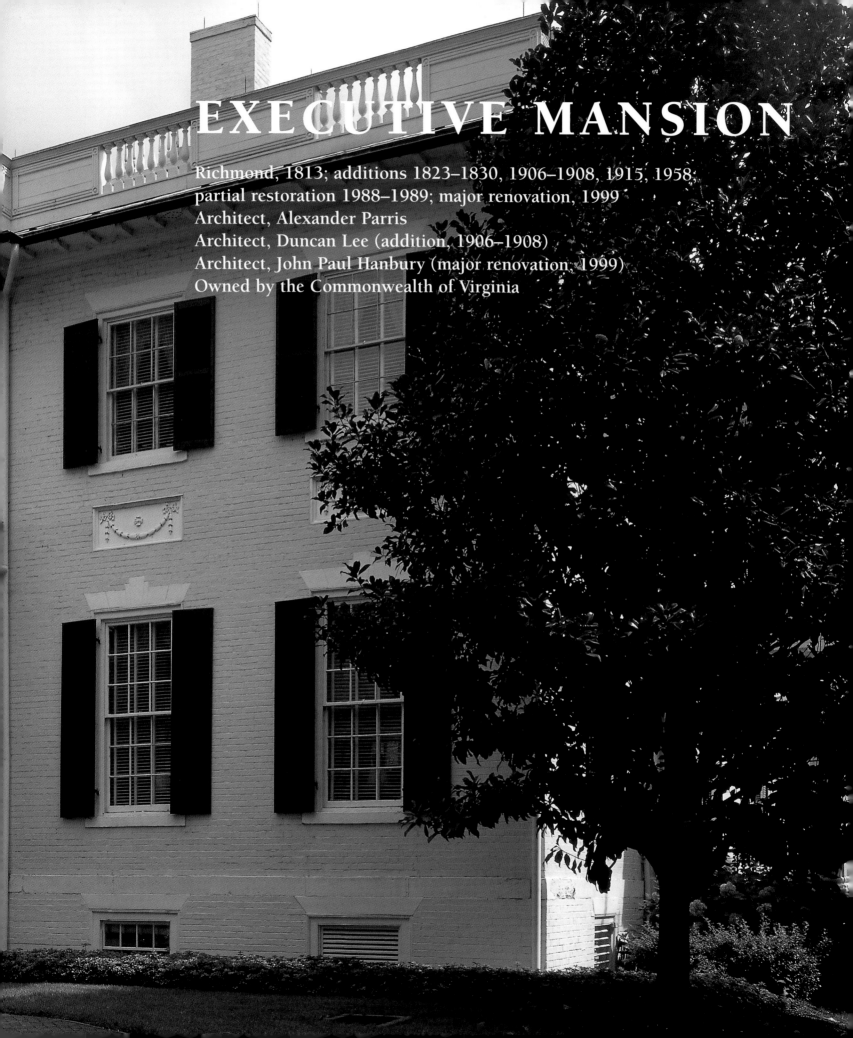

EXECUTIVE MANSION

Richmond, 1813; additions 1823–1830, 1906–1908, 1915, 1958;
partial restoration 1988–1989; major renovation, 1999
Architect, Alexander Parris
Architect, Duncan Lee (addition, 1906–1908)
Architect, John Paul Hanbury (major renovation, 1999)
Owned by the Commonwealth of Virginia

PRECEDING PAGES *The Executive Mansion in Richmond is the home of the governor of Virginia. The stately Federal-style house was built in 1813 and has undergone various modifications and a complete renovation in 1999. Public rooms on the mansion's ground floor receive thousands of visitors and foreign dignitaries each year.*

RIGHT *Through graceful arches that give the 15-foot-high entry hall its voluminous presence with their scale and ornate detailing, the procession toward the ballroom and formal dining room has an elegant formality.*

FOLLOWING PAGES *When the formal dining room was built in 1906, the central portion of the main floor was remodeled to create a large ballroom. It is the mansion's main entertainment area and has hosted formal receptions and balls as well as dinners and weddings. The Colonial Revival-style furnishings include two pair of silk-upholstered sofas and English Adam gilt mirrors above the mantels. A magnificent eight-gallon silver punch bowl is displayed on the c. 1800 mahogany leather-top pedestal drum table in the center of the room.*

The Executive Mansion in Richmond is the home of the governor of Virginia. The stately Federal-style mansion was built in 1813 to replace previous governors' residences, the latest of which was an inappropriate deteriorating wooden house. In 1811 Virginia Governor John Tyler, Sr., had requested that the state build a fitting residence, and shortly thereafter the General Assembly appropriated funds. The mansion was designed by architect Alexander Parris, who later became noted for his buildings in Boston. Modifications made from 1906 to 1908 by architect Duncan Lee included the addition of a new state dining room and the creation of a large ballroom from the former dining room and back parlor. The house survived fires in 1865 and 1926 and continued to function as home to the governor of Virginia while Richmond was the capital of The Confederate States of America.

The Executive Mansion is located in Capitol Square, an open area in downtown Richmond on Shockoe Hill overlooking the James River. The centerpiece of the square is the State Capitol building. The capital of Virginia was moved by then Governor Thomas Jefferson from Williamsburg to Richmond in 1780, and by 1788 the new Capitol building, designed by Jefferson after a Roman temple, was occupied. Jefferson originally intended the area surrounding the

ABOVE *The formal state dining room, an addition made by architect Duncan Lee, is an oval shape, whose curve is reiterated in the three-pedestal mahogany Sheraton table. A c. 1800 American Heppelwhite sideboard is positioned below the sixteenth-century portrait. A fifty-piece heirloom silver service from the USS Virginia, made in 1906 by Bailey, Banks & Biddle, is often used.*

Capitol building to resemble the Roman forum, but the design of Capitol Square became more modern with the Federal-style governor's residence in 1813, and landscape plans for a formal park soon thereafter. Landscaper John P. Shields began grading the deeply guttered dirt area surrounding the structures in 1812. Maximilian Godefroy, a French landscape architect from Baltimore, was commissioned in 1816 to create a park-like setting for Capitol Square. His French Baroque plan enclosed the area in a cast-iron fence. The 1850s re-landscape by John Notman, with fountains and paths, created a more romantic, picturesque park. Within the larger Capitol Square, walls now enclose the Executive Mansion's grounds that include the mansion, a former kitchen and servants quarters-turned-guesthouse, a carriage house, and a garden designed in 1954 by landscape architect Charles Gillette.

The public rooms on the Executive Mansion's ground floor now receive thousands of visitors and foreign dignitaries each year. Two front rooms, originally used as the Governor's office and ladies' parlor, have been flawlessly refurbished with interiors faithful to the 1813 period with an exquisite collection of eighteenth and nineteenth century furniture and artwork. Through sweeping arches that give the 15-foot-high entry hall breadth and depth with their scale and refined detailing, the spacious ballroom at the house's center serves as its main entertaining area. On the far side of the hall the formal state dining room is an oval shape that echoes the sweeping curves found elsewhere in the first floor's space. Huge pocket doors separate this addition from the main entertaining area. Rose tones in the portrait of a woman believed to be Queen Elizabeth I, a focal point for the dining room and entry hall, resonate throughout the crisp, luxurious interior decor.

ABOVE *The ladies' parlor, one of two front rooms in the mansion, was used as the First Ladies' reception room as well as a waiting room. It has been refurbished with interiors faithful to the 1813 period. Furnishings include a spinet piano once owned by Governor James Barbour, a c. 1810 gilt over-mantel mirror with three eglomise panels, a c. 1800-1810 mahogany Sheraton sofa, and an English Regency crystal chandelier.*

LEFT *The Governor's office was where governors received visitors and conducted business. Today, early-nineteenth-century furnishings include a c. 1765 block-front desk and corner chair, and a late-eighteenth-century English mahogany terrestrial globe. A land grant signed in 1784 by Patrick Henry is hung above the upholstered eighteenth-century English settee.*

ABOVE *The c. 1829-1830 portrait of Chief Justice John Marshall, painted by Chester Harding, has a place of honor in the entry hall. The portrait is on loan from Washington and Lee University.*

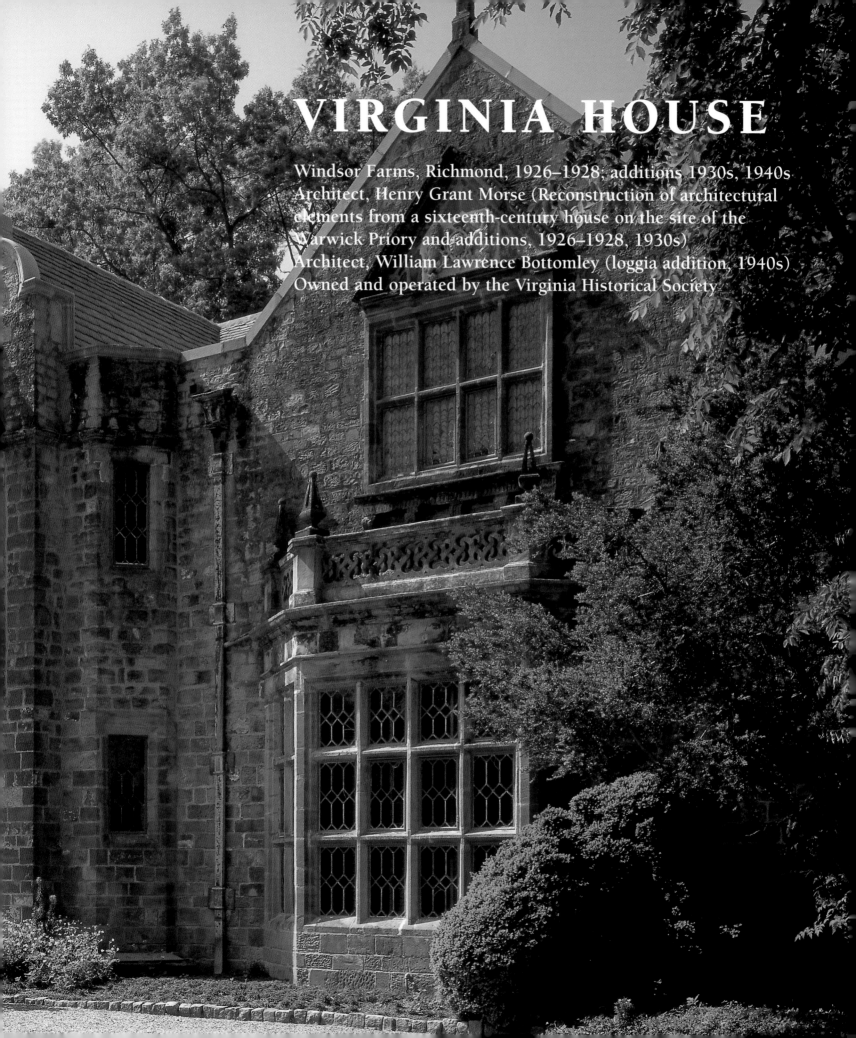

VIRGINIA HOUSE

Windsor Farms, Richmond, 1926–1928; additions 1930s, 1940s
Architect, Henry Grant Morse (Reconstruction of architectural
elements from a sixteenth-century house on the site of the
Warwick Priory and additions, 1926–1928, 1930s)
Architect, William Lawrence Bottomley (loggia addition, 1940s)
Owned and operated by the Virginia Historical Society

PRECEDING PAGES *Virginia House, a stately manor house in Windsor Farms near Richmond, was built during the American country house movement by Alexander and Virginia Weddell as an homage to Mr. Weddell's English ancestry . Architectural elements from a sixteenth-century house known as The Priory in Warwickshire, and other antique timbers, ornamentation, and furnishings were shipped from England and reconstructed on the site near the James River. The Weddells bequeathed Virginia House to the Virginia Historical Society.*

RIGHT *The west wing is a replica of Sulgrave Manor, the Washington family seat in England and the east wing is a replica of the gatehouse and arch at Wormleighton, part of the country seat of the Spencer-Churchill family of Althorp. From the terraced garden, the façade of the manor house glows with antique stone, brick, and stained glass.*

$\mathscr{V}$irginia House, a magnificent stone manor house, is not named as a symbol of its geography but rather after its owner-builder Virginia Weddell. It was completed in 1928 during the revival period in American residential architecture and represents a charming example of the English Gothic style that influenced architecture throughout Europe for centuries. In America the style is especially seen in ecclesiastical and residential structures of the Victorian era and in the revival periods of the 1920s and 1930s. Virginia House's beautiful integration of disparate elements, its quality of materials and craftsmanship, and its visual impact are unique among houses built in America during that latter period.

Virginia House was the residence of well traveled and erudite Alexander and Virginia Weddell. In 1925 Mr. and Mrs. Weddell were the first to purchase one of the larger lots facing the James River in the yet-to-be-developed Windsor Farms, whose mandate for architecture was that it be in the English country style. Since Mr. Weddell was a descendent of George Washington's family, the Weddells planned to travel to England to find plans for Sulgrave Manor, the Washington family seat in Northamptonshire. While in England they attended an auction in Warwickshire, and with great enthusiasm purchased The Priory, a sixteenth-century stone building. They had it dismantled, crated, and shipped to Richmond, and in 1926 began the colossal task of reconstruction, along with other antique architectural pieces, into

PRECEDING PAGES *From the staircase, the great hall's sixteenth-century carved oak elements gleam spectacularly. An electrified late-seventeenth-century Dutch brass chandelier sheds light on the sixteenth- and seventeenth-century portraits, walnut furnishings, and objects d'art purchased for the house by the Weddells.*

LEFT *In the formal dining room, the eighteenth-century Mexican oil-on-canvas folding screen depicts a hunt scene with vivid, warm colors. Furnishings include a late-seventeenth-century English oak chest with inlaid bone and mother-of-pearl ornamentation to the right of the door and a seventeenth-century English oak court or livery cupboard, small and rare, to the left. In the great hall seen through the doorway are highly carved seventeenth-century mahogany choir stalls from Mexico City.*

ABOVE *Romayne panels depicting lords and ladies occupy an upper register of the paneling to one side of the doorway from the great hall to the dining room. (The Weddells had Romaynes of themselves carved in Mexico for each side of the front door in the great hall.) A plaster ceiling depicting animals and the Tudor rose from Elizabeth I's coat of arms was the twentieth-century work of Italian artisans. A portrait of Mr. Weddell in his academic robes hangs above the mantel.*

a cohesive whole. The Weddell's manor house was refashioned with the architectural elements of The Priory as its center section under the professional guidance of architect Henry Grant Morse. Morse incorporated a replica of the Tudor period (circa 1540) Sulgrave Manor into his final design of Virginia House with creation of the west wing. A loggia was added later, designed in the 1940s by architect William Lawrence Bottomley, using antique stone columns that the Weddells had purchased in Granada, Spain, while Mr. Weddell was ambassador to that country.

Virginia House's breathtaking landscape, ambitious both in its scope and diversity, is the result of a 20-year collaboration between Mrs. Weddell and noted landscape architect Charles Gillette. Formal water gardens filled with thousands of lush flowering plants surround fountains and paved terraces, and pathways with stone balustrades carved to Gothic perfection create a wondrous spectacle that cascades over eight acres down to the James River. Only such a scene could complement the grandeur of the ancient stone edifice.

The history, architecture, and gardens of Virginia House are rivaled by its astounding interiors. Architectural details such as the stained glass windows, the Great Room's grand staircase, and carved wall paneling are all antique treasures acquired for the house by the Weddells on their travels. These elements create a dramatic setting of rich historical reference for an outstanding collection of art and furnishings.

The Weddells bequeathed Virginia House to the Virginia Historical Society for the public's pleasure and edification. The society's charge has been well met and Virginia House is one of Richmond's most valued, interesting, and well-visited sources of architectural history.

ABOVE *In the drawing room, sixteenth-century oak pieces used for the paneling of the mantel surround and chimney breast were worked at different periods but blend together seamlessly. The three armorial panels of the chimney breast are nineteenth century, while the date of 1561 is carved into the cartouche of the mantel surround. Fine antiques, such as the eighteenth-century upholstered English wing chair and the late-seventeenth-century oak tea table that holds a pair of sterling silver vermeil footed, covered steeple cups, were purchased to complement the house's historic architecture.*

ABOVE *The loggia was designed by William Lawrence Bottomley from 1944–1946 with disparate elements that included stone columns that the Weddells had purchased in Granada, Spain, as well as finials, a balustrade, and a cornice. With its many stone elements, Bottomley's successful design is an open-air transition between the side garden and the stone manor house.*

RIGHT *Eight acres of exquisite terraced gardens complement the beautiful manor house. They are the creation of a twenty-year collaboration between Virginia Weddell and landscape architect Charles Gillette. From any vantage point the view to the James River is breathtaking.*

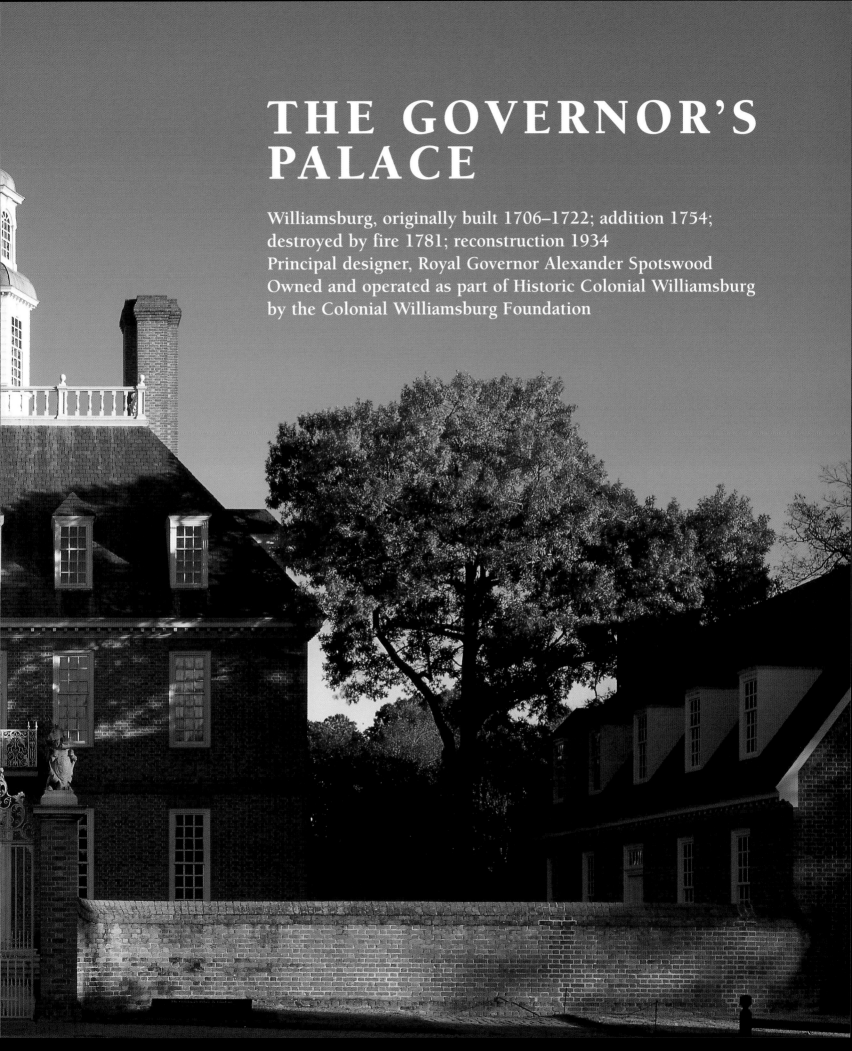

THE GOVERNOR'S PALACE

Williamsburg, originally built 1706–1722; addition 1754;
destroyed by fire 1781; reconstruction 1934
Principal designer, Royal Governor Alexander Spotswood
Owned and operated as part of Historic Colonial Williamsburg
by the Colonial Williamsburg Foundation

PRECEDING PAGES *The Governor's Palace in Williamsburg was reconstructed in 1934 as the centerpiece of the most comprehensive architectural restoration project in American history. The body of the original house was completed by the time royal Governor Alexander Spotswood arrived in 1711. He fired the principal contractor Henry Cary, Sr., and assumed control of the construction of the interiors and gardens of the impressive house, the design of which was meant to reinforce the authority of the English crown's official representative.*

ABOVE *Everything about the governor's house was splendid, fashionable, and expensive. The wrought-iron entrance gates facing the Palace Green are painted and embellished with gold gilt. After 1720, citizens of Williamsburg began to call the house a "palace" because of its opulence.*

OPPOSITE *The formal gardens, the architecture of the house, and the overall site plan of the complex reveal designs of strict Georgian symmetry. A ballroom and supper room were added to the palace in the early 1750s. Designers of the 1934 reconstruction included a gold gilt coat of arms that embellishes the north facade.*

The magnificent Governor's Palace in Williamsburg was reconstructed as part of the most remarkable and comprehensive architectural restoration project in American history. This enormous plan to recreate an important slice of colonial America began with the vision of Reverend Dr. W.A.R. Goodwin of Williamsburg's Bruton Parish Church, and became reality with the passion and focus of one of America's greatest philanthropists and champion of historic preservation, John D. Rockefeller, Jr. With their talents, Williamsburg would rise like a phoenix from the ashes to become a seminal force in the America Colonial Revival movement and an inspiration for future generations.

During the eighty years that Williamsburg was the bustling capital of Virginia, the largest and wealthiest of the colonies, its three defining buildings were the Capitol, the College of

William and Mary, and the Governor's Palace. The grand architecture and gardens of the Palace, situated within a park-like 63 acres of city property, were meant to inspire awe. From 1710 to 1722 royal Governor Alexander Spotswood masterminded the design and supervised the construction of an impressive house that reinforced the power, authority, and elevated status of the English crown's official representative. Together with elaborate gardens that Spotswood privately funded, the glorious mansion, with its sophisticated architecture and well-appointed interiors, was a fitting residence for the most powerful man in colonial America. After the American Revolution the palace served as the official residence during the terms of the first two governors of the Commonwealth of Virginia, Patrick Henry, and Thomas Jefferson. It would burn to the ground in 1781, a year after the capital had been moved to Richmond.

When it was no longer Virginia's seat of government, Williamsburg entered into a long and gradual period of decline. This was halted in the 1920s with commencement of Rockefeller and Goodwin's plan for the once-glorious town's

RIGHT *The central front room on the second floor was large and meant to impress, with its expensive design of tooled and gilded leather covering the walls, beautiful furnishings, and draperies of luxurious crimson damask. The room is reinterpreted as the reception room of the last royal governor's wife, Lady Dunmore. Only the most important visitors were invited into this inner sanctum.* Photograph courtesy The Colonial Williamsburg Foundation.

ABOVE *Double doors at the back of the voluminous and elegant ballroom give access to the supper room, which acted as a saloon. The room is now interpreted with its walls the historically accurate, striking verdigris, one of the most expensive and elegant colors of paint in the eighteenth century.* Photograph courtesy The Colonial Williamsburg Foundation.

rebirth. They believed an accurate representation of the eighteenth-century capital city that had been the epicenter of the political events and social interchanges that had changed the world could be a viable educational and research center for American history. For over thirty years Rockefeller dedicated himself and his fortune to the successful recreation of eighteenth-century Williamsburg, a pursuit that would cost him more than $68 million dollars.

Rockefeller and his talented team of professionals from every discipline of architectural preservation proceeded with the restoration or reconstruction of over a hundred public buildings and residences to recreate an entire historic town, modified only with an infrastructure that provided for modern conveniences. The Governor's Palace was to be rebuilt on

ABOVE *Highly ornate woodwork, such as this curved pediment and escutcheon with the royal arms over the north double door, and the spaciousness of the room, accentuated by its tall coved ceiling, made the palace ballroom the most spectacular entertainment center in the colonies.*

LEFT *The ballroom of the Governor's Palace was added in 1750. It was renowned as one of the colonies' most spacious and elegant centers of entertaining.* Photograph courtesy The Colonial Williamsburg Foundation.

the original foundation using as a design guide a 1730 etching of the building found among documents in the Bodleian Library of Oxford University. The Palace and the other restored or reconstructed buildings now comprise Historic Colonial Williamsburg, a national treasure and an unequaled educational experience realized through its architecture, living history interpretive programs, research facilities, and since 1970 the ongoing work of the Colonial Williamsburg Foundation.

ABOVE AND RIGHT *The maze and manicured formal gardens at the palace were an important extension of the design of the Georgian house. These formally landscaped gardens were part of the 63-acre park in which the palace was situated. Evidence for part of the design appears in the 1730s copperplate engraving of the Governor's Palace.*

MILBURNE

Windsor Farms, Richmond, 1933–1935
Architect, William Lawrence Bottomley
Owned by Mr. and Mrs. William J. Armfield IV

PRECEDING PAGES *Milburne, c. 1935, is one of the most graceful and sophisticated of architect William Lawrence Bottomley's Colonial Revival designs. Wrought-iron gates and a high brick wall provide a befitting stately entrance. The house's formal entrance is a well-proportioned design with a seven-bay façade set off by a central pedimented pavilion.*

RIGHT *The arcades on the wings of the main house are revealed on its garden façade, which faces the James River. Landscaping of the five-acre estate, conceived by architect Bottomley to incorporate terraces, flowering plants, and towering trees, creates a secluded private world minutes from a major city.*

$\mathscr{M}$ilburne, completed near Richmond in 1935, is the epitome of grace among the twentieth-century houses built across America in the popular Colonial Revival style. Its sophisticated and well-informed design draws its inspiration from several of Virginia's great eighteenth-century plantation houses. Milburne was designed by the acclaimed architect William Lawrence Bottomley who became well-known for his masterful interpretations of the Georgian style during the American Colonial Revival movement of the first half of the twentieth century. His work at that time also included numerous other projects in Richmond, such as his Monument Avenue town houses.

Bottomley was hired by former Ambassador and Mrs. Walter S. Robertson to design their new residence in Windsor Farms, an exclusive subdivision that was originally envisioned as a residential park resembling an English village. Bottomley's masterful site plan and creative design resulted in a house that remains not only a perfect expression of a genre but rivals its eighteenth-century models in stateliness and beauty. The popularity of Milburne and other fine Bottomley projects, all built in collaboration with the contracting firm of Claiborne and Taylor, Inc., changed the overall appearance of

PRECEDING PAGES *Bottomley's mastery of proportion and detail are evident in the elliptical-shaped entrance hall's sweeping cantilevered staircase and masterfully carved woodwork. Deeply set double doors that lead to the formal drawing room are centered in the room and aligned with the front door.*

LEFT *The large rectangular formal drawing room features skillfully executed classical detailing that includes fluted Doric pilasters, a Corinthian order modillion cornice, and a pedimented door. The Armfields' fine furnishings and interior design are a perfect complement to the room's elegant character.*

ABOVE *A leaded transom over the double doors leading into the drawing room is an elegant detail that gives extra height to the entry. In the drawing room beyond, an intricately carved garland, centered between the pearwood mantel's carved brackets, is a charming element that lends the room another touch of refinement and beauty.*

ABOVE *The dining room, filled with light from its two large windows facing the James River, is made stately by its modillion cornice, Ionic pilasters, and pedimented doorways. All of the room's carving was executed by New York artisans. Their skill is especially evident in the mantel with its flanking scrolled consoles and the shell carving in its central tablet.*

Windsor Farms into an enclave with many houses designed in the Colonial Revival style.

Milburne's design exemplifies Bottomley's superiority in creative site planning. The five-acre parcel on which it is built is a wedge shape, the apex of which faces the end of a cul-de-sac and the base of which flares out toward the James River. Bottomley set the large brick house far enough back from the road to afford an elegant entry. Wrought-iron gates set into a high brick wall open into a commodious brick-paved motor court, creating an enclosed world for Milburne with the feeling of a private country estate. The broad façade of the mansion closely follows a scheme by the eighteenth-century architect James Gibbs, who took inspiration for his designs from Palladio.

Milburne's beautifully proportioned scale and massing and precise detailing of hand-made brick and carved wood ornamentation are complemented by a simple landscape plan.

Conceived by Bottomley, the plan was executed and elaborated upon by Arthur A. Shurcliff and Alden Hopkins, landscape consultants to Colonial Williamsburg, and later by noted landscape architect Charles A. Gillette. The landscaped gardens create privacy and a sense of seclusion, with many towering trees, formal parterred gardens, and graceful terraced lawns that lead to a vista of the James River. Jane Armfield, a grandchild of the contractor Herbert Claiborne, and her husband William are now Milburne's owners. Jane recalls, "I knew this house growing up and always loved it. But never in my wildest dreams did I think that I would ever live here. It is such a privilege to experience this magical place and I fall in love with it every day." The Armfields' recently redecorated interiors are necessarily comfortable for an active family, yet are appropriately luxurious and reveal a sensitivity to and respect for the house's original character and its place in American architectural history.

ABOVE *In the library, fully paneled walls in sycamore include an unusual scheme wherein the four bookcases set into the walls add a dimension of depth, and numerous full-height Doric pilasters supporting a full entablature with pulvinated frieze add visual height. The Armfields' choice of furnishings and many references to family also add to the room's warm, congenial atmosphere.*

FOLLOWING PAGES *Although a fire in 1942 destroyed half of the woods, the landscape today is mature and lush. At the upper terrace level, the view of the James River as seen from the east garden's English-design, openwork balustrade is expansive and majestic.*

DIRECTORY OF HOUSE MUSEUMS
AND NON-PROFIT ORGANIZATIONS

ARLINGTON HOUSE
George Washington Memorial Parkway
Turkey Run Park
McLean, VA 22101
(703) 235-1530
www.nps.gov/arho

APVA PRESERVATION VIRGINIA
204 West Franklin Street
Richmond, VA 23220
804-648-1889
www.apva.org

BERKELEY
12602 Harrison Landing Road
Charles City, VA 23030
(804) 829-6018; (888) 466-6018
www.berkeleyplantation.com

CARLYLE HOUSE
121 N. Fairfax Street
Alexandria, VA 22314
(703) 549-2997
www.carlylehouse.org

CARTER HALL
255 Carter Hall Lane
Millwood, VA 22646
(540) 837-2100
www.carterhallconferences.org

CLARKE COUNTY HISTORICAL ASSOCIA-
TION
32 Main Street
P.O. Box 306
Berryville, VA 22611
(540) 955-2600
www.clarkehistory.org

THE EXECUTIVE MANSION
Capitol Square
Richmond, VA 23219
(804) 371-8687
executivemansion@governor.virginia.gov

EYRE HALL
Private
See schedule of Historic Garden Week in
Virginia

GLEN BURNIE
901 Amherst Street
Winchester, VA 22601
(540) 662-1473; (888) 556-5799
www.shenandoahmuseum.org.

THE GOVERNOR'S PALACE
Williamsburg, VA
(800) HISTORY
www.colonialwilliamsburg.com

GUNSTON HALL.
10709 Gunston Road
Mason Neck, VA 22079
(703) 550-9220
www.gunstonhall.org.

HISTORIC GARDEN WEEK IN VIRGINIA
12 East Franklin Street
Richmond, VA 23219
(804) 644-7776
www.vagardenweek.org

THE JOHN MARSHALL HOUSE
818 East Marshall Street
Richmond, VA 23219
(804) 648-7998
www.apva.org/marshall

LONG BRANCH
P.O. Box 241
Millwood, VA 22646
(540) 837-1856
www.historiclongbranch.com.

MILBURNE
Private
See schedule for Historic Garden Week in
Virginia.

MONTICELLO
P. O. Box 316
Charlottesville, VA 22902
(434) 984-9822
www.monticello.org

MOUNT AIRY
Private

MOUNT VERNON
3200 Mount Vernon Memorial Highway
Mount Vernon, VA 22121
(703) 780-2000
www.mountvernon.org

NATIONAL TRUST
FOR HISTORIC PRESERVATION
1785 Massachusetts Avenue
N.W., Washington D.C. 20036
(800) 944-6847
www.nationaltrust.org.

OATLANDS
20850 Oatlands Plantation Lane
Leesburg, VA 20175
(703) 777-3174
www.oatlands.org

PROJECT HOPE
255 Carter Hall Lane
Millwood, VA 22646
(540) 837-2100; (800) 544-4673
www.projecthope.org

SHIRLEY
501 Shirley Plantation Road
Charles City, VA 23030
(800) 232-1613
www.shirleyplantation.com

STRATFORD HALL
485 Great House Road
Stratford, VA 22558
(804) 493-8038
www.stratfordhall.org.

TUCKAHOE
Private
See schedule of Historic Garden Week
in Virginia.

VIRGINIA HISTORICAL SOCIETY
428 North Boulevard
P.O. Box 7311
Richmond, VA 23221-0311
(804) 358-4901
www.vahistorical.org

VIRGINIA HOUSE
4301 Sulgrave Road
Richmond, VA. 23221
(804) 353-4251

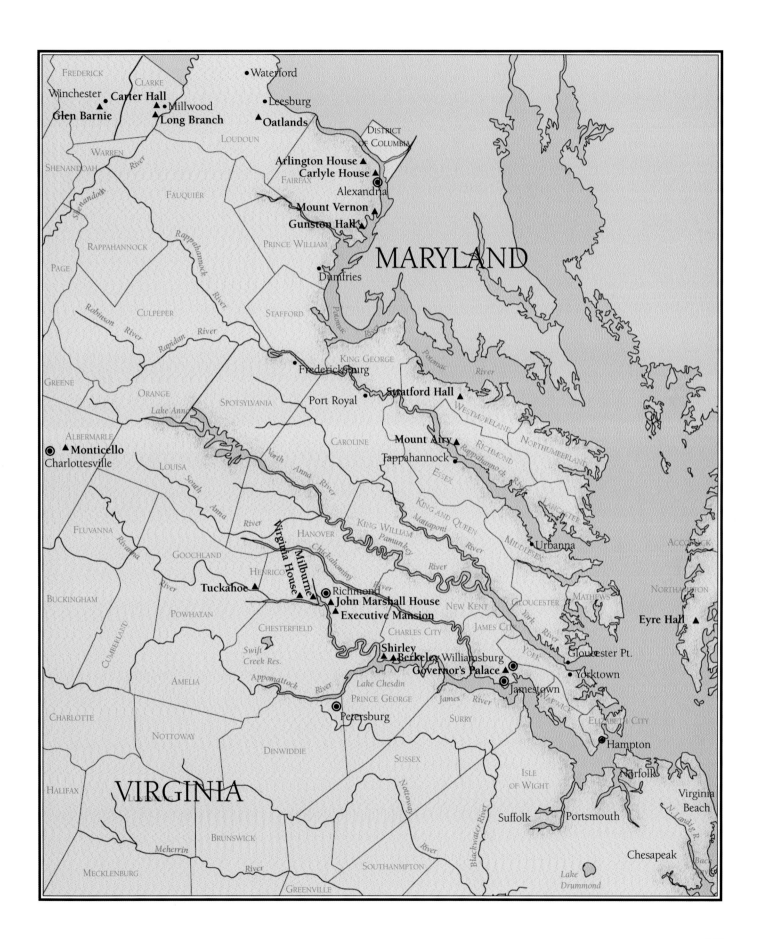

FREDERICK

Winchester • **Carter Hall** ▲

CLARKE

Glen Barnie ▲ ▲ •Millwood
Long Branch

• Waterford

• Leesburg

▲ •Oatlands

DISTRICT
OF COLUMBIA

LOUDOUN

WARREN

SHENANDOAH

Shenandoah

River

Arlington House ▲

Carlyle House ▲
◉
Alexandria

FAIRFAX

FAUQUIER

Rappahannock

Mount Vernon ◄ ▲

Gunston Hall ▲

RAPPAHANNOCK

PRINCE WILLIAM

MARYLAND

PAGE

Robinson

River

CULPEPER

Rapidan

River

• Dumfries

STAFFORD

Potomac

River

KING GEORGE

Potomac

River

GREENE

ORANGE

• Fredericksburg

SPOTSYLVANIA

Lake Anna

• Port Royal •

Stratford Hall ▲

WESTMORELAND

NORTHUMBERLAND

ALBERMARLE

◉ ▲**Monticello**
Charlottesville

LOUISA

North

Anna

River

CAROLINE

Mount Airy ▲

Tappahannock •

RICHMOND

Rappahannock

River

ESSEX

South

Anna

River

KING AND QUEEN

Mattaponi

River

LANCASTER

FLUVANNA

Rivanna

River

HANOVER

KING WILLIAM

Pamunkey

River

MIDDLESEX

• Urbanna

ACCOMACK

GOOCHLAND

Virginia
House

Milburne

Chickahominy

River

River

NORTHAMPTON

BUCKINGHAM

HENRICO

Tuckahoe ▲

◉ Richmond

John Marshall House ▲

Executive Mansion ▲

NEW KENT

JAMES CITY

GLOUCESTER

York

River

MATHEWS

Eyre Hall ▲

POWHATAN

CHESTERFIELD

Swift
Creek Res.

CHARLES CITY

Shirley ▲

▲ **Berkeley** • Williamsburg

Governor's Palace ▲ ◉

Gloucester Pt.

CUMBERLAND

AMELIA

Appomattock

River

Lake Chesdin

James

River

◉
Jamestown

York

River

• Yorktown

CHARLOTTE

PRINCE GEORGE

SURRY

NANSICK

ELIZABETH CITY

NOTTOWAY

◉
Petersburg

DINWIDDIE

James River

ISLE
OF WIGHT

• Hampton

Norfolk

Virginia
Beach

VIRGINIA

HALIFAX

SUSSEX

Nottoway

River

Suffolk

Portsmouth

N. Landis. R.

BRUNSWICK

Meherrin

River

SOUTHAMPTON

River

Blackwater River

Chesapeak

Back
River

MECKLENBURG

GREENVILLE

Lake
Drummond

RESOURCES

Bear, James A., Jr., ed. *Jefferson at Monticello*. Charlottesville: University Press of Virginia, 1967.

Brodie, Fawn. *Thomas Jefferson, An Intimate History*. New York: Bantam Books, Inc., 1974.

Brown, Stuart E., Jr., and Ann Barton Brown. *Carter Hall and the Civil War*. Berryville, Virginia: Virginia Book Company, 2003.

Cornforth, John. *Early Georgian Interiors*. New Haven: Yale University Press, 2004.

Dowdey, Clifford. *The Great Plantation, A Profile of Berkeley Hundred and Plantation Virginia from Jamestown to Appomattox*. Charles City, Virginia: Berkeley Plantation, 1976.

Fallin, Catherine. *Chesapeake, The Eastern Shore Gardens and Houses*. New York: Simon & Schuster, 1993.

Garrett, Wendell, ed. *George Washington's Mount Vernon*. New York: The Monacelli Press, Inc., 1998.

Griswold, Mac. *Washington's Gardens at Mount Vernon: Landscape of the Inner Man*. Boston: Houghton Mifflin Company, 1999.

Halliday, E.M. *Understanding Thomas Jefferson*. New York: HarperCollins Publishers, Inc., 2001.

Hosmer, Charles B., Jr. *Presence of the Past, A History of the Preservation Movement in the United States before Williamsburg*. New York: G. P. Putnam's Sons, 1965.

Isaac, Rhys. *The Transformation of Virginia 1740-1790*. United States of America: The University of North Carolina Press, 1999.

Johnson, Paul. *George Washington, The Founding Father*. New York: HarperCollins Publishers, 2005.

Kilmer, Kenton, and Donald Sweig. *The Fairfax Family in Fairfax County*. Fairfax: The Fairfax County Office of Comprehensive Planning Under the Direction of the County Board of Supervisors in Cooperation with the County History Commission, 1975.

Kimball, Fiske. *Domestic Architecture of the American Colonies and of the Early Republic*. New York: Charles Scribner's Sons, 1922. Reprint, Mineola, New York: Dover Publications, Inc., 2001.

Kopper, Philip. *Colonial Williamsburg*, rev. ed. New York: Harry N. Abrams, Inc., in association with The Colonial Williamsburg Foundation, 2001.

Krusen, Jessie Ball Thompson. *Tuckahoe Plantation*. Richmond, Virginia: Whittet & Shepperson, 1975.

Lathrop, Elise. *Historic Houses of Early America*. New York: Tudor Publishing, 1941.

Leath, Robert A., and Betty C. Leviner. "A Proposal for Revisions to the John Carlyle House Historic Furnishings Plan." Alexandria, Virginia: Northern Virginia Regional Park Authority, 2005.

Leepson, Marc. *Saving Monticello, The Levy Family's Epic Quest to Rescue the House That Jefferson Built*. New York: The Free Press, A Division of Simon & Schuster, Inc., 2001.

Lehmann, Karl. *Thomas Jefferson, American Humanist*. Charlottesville: University Press of Virginia, 1985.

Loth, Calder, ed. *The Virginia Landmarks Register*, Fourth Edition. Charlottesville and London: The University Press of Virginia, 1999.

Mapp, Alf J., Jr. *The Faith of Our Fathers, What America's Founders Really Believed*. New York: Rowman & Littlefield Publishers, Inc., 2003.

Miles, Daniel W.H. "The Tree-Ring Dating of Eyre Hall, Cheriton, Northampton County, Virginia." Oxfordshire, England: Oxford Dendrochronology Laboratory, April 2003.

Munson, James D. Col. *John Carlyle, Gent., A True and Just Account of the Man and His House*. Alexandria, Virginia: Northern Virginia Regional Park Authority, 1986.

Nelligan, Murray H., Ph.D. *Arlington House, The Story of the Robert E. Lee Memorial*. Burke, Virginia: Chatelaine Press, 1953, 2001.

O'Neal, William Bainter, and Christopher Weeks. *The Work of William Lawrence Bottomley in Richmond*. Charlottesville: University Press of Virginia, 1985.

Price, David A. *Love and Hate in Jamestown, John Smith, Pocahontas, and the Start of a New Nation*. New York: Vintage Books, Random House, Inc., 2003.

Rasmussen, William M.S., and Robert S. Tilton. *Old Virginia: The Pursuit of a Pastoral Ideal*. Charlottesville: Howell Press, 2003.

Roberts, Bruce. *Plantation Homes of the James River*. Chapel Hill: The University of North Carolina Press, 1990.

Ross, Charles L. 1989. "Historic Significance: Eyre Hall's Virginia Legacy." *Veranda III* (3): 122-129.

Rothery, Agnes. *Houses Virginians Have Loved*. New York: Rinehart & Company, Inc.; Toronto: Clarke, Irwin & Company, Ltd, 1954.

Seale, William. *Virginia's Executive Mansion*. Richmond: The Virginia State Library and Archives, 1988.

Virginia Historic Landmarks Commission and Historic American Buildings Survey, Compilers. *Virginia Catalog, A List of Measured Drawings, Photographs, and Written Documentation in the Survey*. Charlottesville: University of Virginia Press, 1976.

Waterman, Thomas Tileston. *The Mansions of Virginia 1706-1776*. New York: Bonanza Books, University of North Carolina Press, 1945.

Wells, Camille. "Virginia By Design: The Making of Tuckahoe and the Remaking of Monticello," ARRIS: Journal of the Southeast Chapter of the Society of Architectural Historians 12, (2001).

Wilkins, Roger. *Jefferson's Pillow, The Founding Fathers and the Dilemma of Black Patriotism*. Boston: Beacon Press, 2001.

Young, Joanne. *Shirley Plantation, A Personal Adventure for Ten Generations*. Charles City County, Virginia: Shirley Plantation, 1981.

ACKNOWLEDGMENTS

To the generations of African Americans, who as slaves with sufferance and ingenuity, built most of these magnificent houses and who, as co-creators of America, enabled our founding fathers to pursue their intellectual curiosities, act on their convictions, and build our free nation.

Arlington House, The Robert E. Lee Memorial, Arlington

APVA Preservation Virginia. Catherine Dean, Curator of Collections; Benjamin Knowles, Image Bank, Richmond

Mr. and Mrs. William J. Armfield IV, Richmond

H. Furlong Baldwin, Eyre Hall, Northampton County

Berkeley. The Jamieson family, owners; Tammy Radcliff, Office Manager; Mattie Jones, Historical Interpreter; Jim Curtis, Historical Interpreter, Charles City, Charles City County

Carlyle House Historic Park. Mary Ruth Coleman, Administrator; Jim Bartlinski, Curator, Alexandria

Carter Hall. Millwood, Clarke County

Carter Hall Conference Center (The). Project HOPE, The People-to-People Health Foundation, Inc., Millwood, Clarke County

Roger Chavez, Burwell-Morgan Mill, Millwood

Childs F. Burden, Middleburg

Mrs. Herbert A. Claiborne, Jr., Richmond

Clarke County Historical Association. Jennifer Lee, Executive Director, Berryville, Clarke County

Colonial Williamsburg Foundation. Jim Bradley, Public Relations Manager; Carl Lounsbury, Architectural Historian; Robert Leath, Curator, Historic Interiors

Marcia Cronan, Delaplane

Daniel and Company, Inc. Samuel W. Daniel, President and CEO, Richmond

Executive Mansion. Amy E. Bridge, Director; former First Lady Roxane Gilmore, Chair, Executive Mansion Renovation Project; Asha Holloman, Assistant to Director; Martin "Tutti" Townes, Butler, Richmond

Foundation for Historic Christ Church. Robert Cornelius, Executive Vice President; Robert Teagle, Education Director, Irvington, Lancaster County

Friends of Poplar Forest, The Corporation for Thomas Jefferson's Poplar Forest, Forest, Bedford County

Friends of the Hollow: Boyhood Home of Chief Justice John Marshall. Thomas Marshall deButts, President, Arlington

Garden Club of Virginia (The), Richmond

Glen Burnie Historic House & Gardens, Winchester, Frederick County

Gunston Hall. David L. Reese, Executive Director; Susan C. Blankenship, Development Coordinator, Mason's Neck, Fairfax County

Hanbury Evans Newill Vlattas. John Paul Hanbury, F.A.I.A.; Barbara Strickland-Page, Principal Designer, Norfolk

Louise Hayman, Annapolis, Maryland

Historic Long Branch House Museum and Farm. Colette Poisson, Curator, Millwood, Clarke County

James Madison's Montpelier, The Montpelier Foundation. Michael Quinn, Executive Director; Lee Langston-Harrison, Director of Curatorial Operations; Sandy Mudrinish, Horticulturalist, Montpelier Station, Orange County

John Marshall House. Catherine Dean, Curator of Collections APVA Preservation Virginia; Patricia Archer, former Site Coordinator, Richmond

Calder Loth, Sr. Architectural Historian, Virginia Department of Historic Resources, Richmond

Monticello, the Thomas Jefferson Foundation, Inc. Daniel P. Jordon, President; Wayne Mogielnicki, Director of Communications; Elizabeth Chew, Ph.D., Associate Curator of Collections; Kat Imhoff, Vice President of Planning and Facilities, Charlottesville, Albemarle County

Josephine, Esme, Camille Morris, Delaplane

Mount Vernon: George Washington's Estate & Gardens. James Rees, Executive Director; Linda Ayres, Associate Director of Collections; Stephanie Pace Brown, Associate Director of Public Affairs; Gretchen M. Goodell, Assistant Curator; Justin Gunther, Manager of Restoration; Julia Moseley, Retail Manager; Dennis Pogue, Director for Preservation; Mary Thompson, Research Specialist; Melissa Wood, Media Relations Associate, Fairfax County

Museum of the Shenandoah Valley (Glen Burnie Historic House & Gardens). Jennifer Esler, Executive Director; Julie B. Armel, Public Relations/Marketing Coordinator; Frances W. Crawford, Director of Development; Leila Boyer, Research Historian, Winchester, Frederick County

National Park Service, Department of the Interior, United States of America. Arlington House, The Robert E. Lee Memorial. Laura Anderson, Curator; Deborah Deas, Administration; Matthew Penrod, Ranger and Interpreter; Kendell Thompson, Site Manager

Anne Neuman, Richmond County

Oatlands. David V. Boyce, Executive Director; Elizabeth Simon, House Manager; B.J. Mahoney, Director of Grounds, Buildings, Security and Maintenance; Carole Greetham, Accounts, Leesburg, Loudoun County

David Pashley, American Bird Conservancy, The Plains

Project HOPE/The People-to-People Health Foundation, Inc. (at Carter Hall). John P. Howe, III, M.D., President & CEO; Lori Allesee, Director of Communications; Deborah H. Carl, Vice President Human Resources & Administration; Burt Kaplan, Director of Facilities Services; Mary Nokes, Sales and Marketing Manager

Cheryl Hanback Shepherd, Architectural Historian, Millennium Preservation Services, Warrenton

Gavin Shire, American Bird Conservancy, The Plains

Shirley. Charles Hill Carter, Jr., Owner; Janet L. Appel, Director; Christine Crumlish Joyce, Curator, Charles City, Charles City County

Francoise Skurman, San Francisco

Rick Stoutamyer, Undercover Books, Marshall

Stratford Hall. Robert E. Lee Memorial Association, Inc. Jim Schepmoes, Director of Marketing and Public Relations; Judy Hynson, Chief Interpreter, Stratford, Westmoreland County

Mrs. H. Gwynne Tayloe, Jr., Mount Airy, Richmond County, Northern Neck

Thomas Jefferson's Poplar Forest, Bedford County

Tommy's Garden. Tommy Autry, Florist, Richmond

Tuckahoe. Addison B. Thompson, JD, Sagemark Consulting, Glen Allen, and Sue Thompson, owner-managers; Hannah Warfield, Gardener; Mrs. Evelyn Harris, Housekeeper, Goochland County

Virginia Historical Society. Muriel B. Rogers, Ph. D., Curator of Special Projects and Virginia House, Richmond

Virginia House, Richmond

Richard Guy Wilson, Ph.D., Commonwealth Professor and Chair, Architectural History, School of Architecture, University of Virginia, Charlottesville

Alex and Hana Young, American Bird Conservancy

INDEX